THE SEVEN GIFTS

THE SEVEN GIFTS

BERNARD J. KELLY, C.S.Sp.

NEW YORK
SHEED & WARD
MCMXLII

FIRST PUBLISHED SEPTEMBER 1941
BY SHEED AND WARD, LTD.
FROM 110/111 FLEET STREET
LONDON, E.C.4

PERMISSU SUPERIORUM
ÑIHIL OBSTAT: GEORGIUS D. SMITH, S.TH.D.
CENSOR DEPUTATUS
IMPRIMATUR: E. MORROGH BERNARD
VIC. GEN.
WESTMONASTERII, DIE 26ª JUNII 1941

PRINTED IN THE UNITED STATES OF AMERICA
BY THE POLYGRAPHIC COMPANY OF AMERICA, N.Y.

To
**CHRIST
MY KING**

INTRODUCTION

Modern spiritual writers refer frequently in their works to the gifts of the Holy Ghost in a passing manner. But the number of treatises dealing with the gifts themselves falls far below what the importance thus given them would lead us to expect. It is true that they have been considered at length under certain aspects—most particularly as elements entering into the achievements of man's spiritual perfection in the mystical state. No attempt, however—as far as the knowledge of the present writer goes—has been made to show what they mean in the life of the ordinary Christian. To make this attempt is the purpose of this book.

St Thomas has been followed throughout, although the non-technical character of the treatment renders detailed references out of place. The careful student of St Thomas's thought will notice that where his later statements indicate a clear development beyond the thought of his earlier works, the later view has been accepted and the earlier interpreted in its light. By following this method we have been enabled to enrich St Thomas's definite position with all that is of permanent value in the stages by which he arrived at it.

My sincerest thanks are due to all those who, by correction, suggestion, or material collaboration, contributed to the production of the book. What they did is none the less pleasing to God though being unknown of men.

HOLY GHOST SENIOR SCHOLASTICATE

KIMMAGE

FEAST OF SS. PETER AND PAUL, JUNE 29th, 1940.

CONTENTS

Contents

THE SEVEN GIFTS

THE SEVEN GIFTS

CHAPTER I

SONS OF GOD

"He gave them power to be made the sons of God."
(John i. 12.).

The human mind, we are told by some, progresses ever towards a state of full and perfect knowing, compared with which the condition of the wisest of the ancients will appear to have been but helpless groping. There are others who think that the bankruptcy of man's thought has already made its presence felt. Neither of these positions is necessarily true. Man may be much as he ever was. And the fact that two such contradictory views can be held seems to point neither to man's omniscience nor to his stupidity but rather to the fundamental characteristic of his intellect—its finite nature—which is the ultimate explanation of man's peculiar power of formulating nonsense about truths he has scarce glimpsed.

For whatever be the power of the human mind to penetrate the depths of the physical world and reduce its chaos to the order of scientific schematization, man remains a child in the presence of the great problems of life, and above all else in the presence of the problem of problems—the problem of Him Who gave life. But few have arrived unaided by revelation at coherence. Those few arrived there after patient investigation and along a road strewn with the debris of cast-off hypotheses. If we consider that section of mankind to which revelation has either not at all, or but fragmentarily, penetrated, we may truly say that as a body it has failed to know God even as He may be known by reason, while the God of Faith is in their eyes but folly.

Sad though this may seem, it could not be otherwise. Man as such is the last and lowest of the intellectual creatures of God; fallen man is the slave of the prince of darkness. And hence it is that the sublimest of the truths evade our grasp. The mind cannot in one glance penetrate their content. It is forced to set about its task by taking it bit by bit. Idea after idea is grasped and the whole is not understood save as the sum of its parts. God is the infinite, the eternal, the true, the just; and all these in Him are one and the same thing; but for That Thing we have no name which is not more properly the name of a part.

God Himself has come to our aid and has given us the revelation of faith. We know that God is Three in One; that of the Three, One became man. These and so many other truths were outside the scope of unaided reason. Faith has given reason a new power of knowing, but a power grafted on to reason and respecting some of its essential limitations. Reason cannot see God; neither does Faith see Him. Reason employs man-made ideas; Faith merely extends their field of validity. Reason knows what pertains to God by taking it piecemeal; faith cannot act otherwise. Reason knows God by means of many concepts; faith adds a few more to the list. The God of faith is God seen from many angles: God seen from within is the God of the beautific vision.

Grace raises man to the divine level. Grace is the principle of the life of God as shared in by man. Grace is known only by faith. But faith is a faculty which grasps its object by splitting it up. Here we have the explanation of a fact which may at some time have caused wonder, namely, the extraordinary variety of terms employed to express the state of grace. We speak of grace, of the life of grace, of the life of the theological virtues, of the life of union with Our Lord and His Blessed Mother. By all these terms we mean the same reality. It is the same life which is in question in each case. But this life is something divine, something far above the comprehension of man illumined though he be by faith, and he must perforce grasp it point by point, view it first from one angle and then from another, and finally represent to himself that essentially simple and sublime reality as complex, the resultant of many vital forces. And in the regulation of his personal life he turns from the one idea to the other, at one time endeavouring to be united to Our Lord, and then, when that ceases to excite devotion, turning perhaps to the fact that he has within him a new life which seeks its outlet in acts of virtue. And other than this he cannot do till God take him hand in hand and reduce his life to the unity of love.

There is, however, one idea which is faith's preferred expression of the life of grace, and that is the idea of our divine sonship. St John, in the prologue to his Gospel, sets before us the sum total of the divine scheme of things, and in it man is found as the child of the Most High. "He came unto His own and His own received Him not. But as many as received Him, He gave them power to be made the sons of God" (John i. 11-12). This idea comes nearer than any other to expressing the full import of grace. Every other idea leaves much to be understood. The life of union with Our Lord is possible only to someone who is His brother. It includes then, necessarily, the concept of divine sonship. But it includes it without forcing it upon our notice. Acts of Faith, Hope and Charity are natural only to a son of God. But it is possible to think of them and leave their implication unnoticed. It is not so with the idea of sonship of God. The son of God by grace is necessarily the friend of Him Who is Son of God by nature. The life of the son by grace must be a life of knowledge and love of his adorable Father, of trust in His all-powerful aid. God in revealing our state to us under this image has given us a key to the mystery of our new being, and this key will open to us the treasure of our life "now hid with Christ in God" (Col. iii. 3).

Almighty God has given us the idea of sonship by grace as the fullest and most accurate expression of the spiritual life possible to us while we still wander far from our eternal home. It is in relation to this idea that we are to understand all that faith teaches about the mystery of redeemed and elevated man. This is the centre upon which all the scattered data of revelation seem to focus themselves. This is the point from which every partial glimpse will assume proper perspective. Were we then to wish to obtain a clear idea of the meaning of the gifts of the Holy Ghost and their dynamism in the life of grace we must integrate them into the concept of divine sonship. They have been given to us either because we are sons of God or in order that we may become sons of God or for some other reason connected with the fact that we are now members of the family of Our Creator. To study them in isolation would be to run the risk of never perceiving their true importance. Nothing is isolated in God's works of art. Every item, however minute, is essential to the whole and should be understood in terms of the whole. The nearest approximation to the idea of the whole of what God has done for man is to say that He made him His child.

"Behold," says St John (1 John iii. 1), "what manner of charity the Father hath bestowed upon us that we should be called and should be the sons of God." From all eternity the Father had one Son, equal to Himself, the splendour of His glory and mirror of His perfections. No son has ever been like his father as is the Word like to the First Person of the Most Adorable Trinity. He is not merely like to Him in nature; He has the same nature as the Father. Both possess the same Godhead. Both have the same essential life, the same essential acts of knowledge and love; both unite in the bliss of Their perfect union in that ineffable breathing forth of the Holy Spirit in which is completed the cycle of Trinitarian Life, and the number of Those Who are One God is completed. All that the Father has He gives to the Son. All that the Son has he receives from the Father. Father, Son, and Holy Ghost—Three Divine Persons united in the bliss of the possession of a common happiness, a common life, a common fullness and infinity of being.

And then God made man and poured grace into his soul. Do we realize what that act implied? Within the Godhead there were Three Who possessed the Divinity. There could be no more who would own this Treasure by way of absolute identity with It. But there was still one other possibility. Man could own the Divinity by possessing It as the object of his knowledge and love. God known and God loved constituted God's own riches—all that God held dear in Its own right. And God determined to give this treasure to man—to invite man to community of life and interests with Himself

—to give man a share in What made God's Life the Life of bliss it was. God adopted man into His family and gave him right of entry to His most secret treasure-house.

It is essential for the understanding of man's adoptive sonship that we distinguish it clearly from the natural Sonship of the Word, the Son of the Father, and the sonship by which man is related to man. All sonship is based on similarity and, ultimately, on identity. The son is son of a father in that he has proceeded from him and has the same nature as he has. The father is a man. So also the son. Besides, there are, usually, certain accidental features of resemblance: the son may be of much the same build as his father, have his father's eyes, his hair. There will follow from community of conditions of life, community of spiritual riches. The son will be heir to the philosophy of life won by the father at the price of daily pain. The father will see in the son, perhaps, the as yet clear outlines of what is the stuff that goes to make him, too, up, and knowing his son, will know himself better. And then there will be community of material wealth; for the son is heir to all that the father has.

The Word was Son of the Father, but not just as man is son of man. The Word had not a nature like that of the Father; He had the same, identically the same, Nature as the Father. Never was son so closely united to father as in the Blessed Trinity. There is not just community of spiritual wealth, there is identity; the Mind of the One is the Mind of the Other; the Heart of the One is the Heart of the Other. There is identity of life, of interests, of activity. In the Trinity all is one except personality. The Trinity is Three Persons, One God, One life, One love, One knowledge.

That God in making us His sons did not make of each of us His Word is abundantly clear. Nor is it much more difficult to see that we are not His children either in the way in which we are children of an earthly father. We have the same nature as our fathers according to the flesh—not, of course, the very same nature as they, but one of exactly the same kind. But even grace does not make us of exactly the same kind as God. God is far above all that is and that can be. No one is like unto Him. He inhabiteth light inaccessible and we can but hope to catch the warmth of His rays. There remains but one possibility; that He has given us a share in His treasure and in His power of using it—that He has, in other words, adopted us into His family and given us a right to that heritage which in strict justice would belong only to a natural son. Our sonship of God is an adoptive sonship. He has chosen us freely, lifted us above our condition of merely rational creatures and invited us to participate in the family life of the Three Divine Persons. In His eyes, and in the eyes of the heavenly court, we are now no longer mere creatures. We are members of the family of God and must be evaluated in terms of that dignity.

In speaking of our new relation to God by grace as one of adoptive sonship, we employ a terminology that conveys some idea to even the most ordinary intelligence. Most people have some idea of what is meant by being adopted into a family. They grasp in a general way at least that the adopted child was before adoption fatherless, or at least in straitened circumstances; that by adoption it was raised to a state above the miserable plight in which it had been; that the adoption was an act of mercy and compassion—a purely altruistic gesture of giving without hope of recompense. Whoever under-

stands adoptive sonship in this way has already matter
which will excite him to love of God. He sees the perfect
gratuity of grace, the depths of misery and sin from
which it has raised him, the inexpressible dignity that
is now his. Such ideas suffice for the practical guidance
of life. They furnish an ample incentive to charity and
penance. But they are as yet too vague, too incomplete,
to serve as basis for a theoretical synthesis of Christian
life. If, then, we wish to find the place allotted to the
gifts of the Holy Ghost—and, knowing them better, wish
to submit self more fully to their action—we must clarify
our notion of adoptive sonship, particularly in so far as
it may be applicable to a state of man relative to God.

Adoptive sonship among men consists essentially in
the acceptance of a stranger into community of family
life as a son, and in giving him a certain right to share
in the goods of the family, as is the strict right of one
born into it. Certain modalities may make themselves
felt in certain practical cases. The adoption may be
more or less complete. The right to a share in the family
goods may be limited. The newcomer may—practically
at least—not be accepted on terms of perfect equality.
But it is essential that the principle of each of these two
elements be preserved. A person adopted into a family
without right to its goods is just some kind of a permanent guest. One with this right, but without any status
of equality, is just a privileged servant.

It will, however, be noticed that as a matter of fact
children are usually adopted because of certain natural
qualities which have been theirs by birth. Human
adoption is not perfectly gratuitous. A father adopts
a child into, his family because he has no child of his
own and thinks that the one he intends to adopt is
capable of carrying on the family name and traditions

worthily. Or perhaps the child may be intelligent and well-behaved and deserves a chance. Here there is a very great measure of pure charity. But there are things that the father cannot give. He cannot give the child intelligence and innate good breeding. He can, it is true, perfect the child's natural powers by careful education. But he does not give these natural powers. In fact they are presupposed to all efforts of his. His generosity, however pure it may be, has thus a limit set it. He cannot change the nature of the child. He can adopt only a child born of woman, and the greatest benefit he can confer is the realization of what is already within the child's power by nature, though it may be denied it by accident of birth.

There is still another limit set to the power of man to adopt, and it is akin to the one we have just considered. It is that adoption not only presupposes human nature in the person adopted, but that it is, in addition, a state of which human nature as such is not unworthy. No man can give another something which is far beyond what man has the right to obtain in favourable circumstances. Man can give human riches, a human name, a title to human respect. But all these might have been the lot of the recipient already had he been born to other parents. There is nothing in such things to which man as such is not entitled if events were but slightly different from what they have been. And none of these benefits will make one anything more than a man. They may make a man rich, or powerful, or respected. But they do so by making him into a·rich man or a powerful man or a respected man as the case may be. In no case can they make him more than a man.

Human adoption has then an upper and a lower limit. It presupposes human nature in the person to be adopted;

it can do no more than bring out the best that is latent in that nature. When God adopts into His family such barriers are brushed aside.

Our Lord revealed to us this great secret of divine adoption in the words He spoke one night to Nicodemus: "Amen, amen, I say to thee, unless a man be born again of water and the Holy Ghost, he cannot enter into the kingdom of God" (John iii. 5). To be adopted by God is to receive a new nature. God is so far removed above His creatures that they can never hope to move with ease in His presence—much less hope to live as members of His family—with nothing more than the resources given them by nature. Only a man can share in the family life of a man. Only someone like God can share in God's family life. But no creature is by nature like unto God—unless in a far and indistinct manner. "There is none like to Thee, O Lord: Thou art great and great is Thy Name in might" (Jer. x. 6). Not only then must God give us entry to His family, He must, as well, give us that which makes us capable of being received therein—a share, namely, in His own divine nature through the gift of sanctifying grace. It is by grace, and grace alone—nature cannot lift us up so high —that we have the power of walking in fellowship with God. It is grace which gives us the power of appropriating to our own use the divine treasure of treasures— God Himself brought within our reach as an object we can know and love, as an object upon which we can centre life. To acquire this power is really a new birth. It is no longer the old man of sin and death that is clothed in our flesh, but the new man of grace and life, a new creature sharing in the life of the Most High, capable of uttering words and thinking thoughts which it is not given to man to understand.

It follows from this that the adopted child of God is no longer a mere man: "Jesus answered them: Is it not written in your law: I said you were gods" (John x. 34). Sharing in the very nature of God we are more than man. We count as more than men in the world—though in the eyes of the same world we may seem less than many. For grace has raised us above all that is created. We have been reformed, reshaped by God, born again, not of woman, but of the Holy Ghost. We have entered into the womb of the Most High and the Spirit has breathed upon us the fragrance of a divine life.

There are, however, points in which human adoption throws a positive light on what grace does for the soul. There is, for example, the right adoption gives to a share in the family life and goods of the father. Grace gives the adopted child of God a right to the divine treasure—it gives him even a certain use of this treasure here on earth, as earnest of Its full possession in heaven. And that treasure is God Himself. It seems strange to ears of earth to speak of God as a treasure. A treasure for us is something to have and look at—some kind of a valuable, or just money with which we can get whatever we want. That money as such is not a real treasure is clear; it should be valued only as a means of getting something else. But of what kind should be that something else? Should it be beautiful? God is eternal beauty. Should it give us power? No one is as strong as he who has the Lord as his heritage. Should it be an inexhaustible object upon which to exercise our faculties of intellect and will? God can never be known or loved to excess. God is, in fact, the only real treasure. Whoever has God has all that the heart can desire; without God the soul tastes the bitterness of the void. To know God and to love Him is to possess Him, to have Him so at our disposal that we can turn to Him at any moment and feast upon His infinite perfections. Where the heart is, there is one's treasure. God is a treasure upon which the heart can fix itself in ecstasy.

Grace does not stop at giving a right to the divine heritage as something to be possessed later: it implies a certain possession and enjoyment of God even now. The Holy Ghost, Who is God, is given us by grace. ". . . the charity of God is poured forth in our hearts, by the Holy Ghost, Who is given to us" (Rom. v. 5). He is given to every soul in the state of grace to be known and loved. He inhabits the soul. He reigns there, making it His throne, and awaiting the homage of interest and affection. He is already within our grasp —not so fully as He will be when we shall possess Him in heaven, but none the less really. The child of God possesses God.

There is still one aspect of human adoption which is often taken for granted, but which is the real key to the mystery of the gifts of the Holy Ghost: it is that the adopted child is often of much lower station by birth and early upbringing than the family into which it is received. We all know that this fact is of enormous importance in the practical working out of the details of the child's new life. It may have been used to misery, neglect, indifference, on the part of its elders; its life, even in its tenderest years, may have been a struggle for existence, fought out in a milieu where every hand seemed to be lifted against it. Such a child will not at once fit into its new family life. It doubts the reality of the comfort that surrounds it. It thinks that the new state of affairs cannot last; that there must be deception somewhere. It cannot believe fully in the genuineness of the care and affection that now surround it. Men have hitherto been its enemies, and it cannot at once grasp the fact that man may be a friend and benefactor. The old idea, that every comfort is the fruit of a struggle, and is doomed to be lost in a new struggle with some stronger foe, makes the child selfish, ungrateful, suspicious. In short, its life is as yet but nominally that of one of the family, and this, not because of the fact that full participation in the life of the family has been denied it, but because it is unable of itself to seize and use to the full the opportunities of living presented to it now for the first time.

The relation in which the soul adopted into the family of Almighty God stands to its new Father is a heightened form of that in which a slum child would stand to the most cultured of parents. Man is the lowest of the intellectual beings, the farthest removed from God. If God is above the highest of the angels, and if the highest of the angels cannot without grace elicit the slightest act of knowledge or love of God as He is in Himself, how lower still must not man be and how far removed from God? The slum child has the use of reason and nothing more is needed to fit it for the most refined human life. But it is not capable, in point of fact, of the slightest expression of ease in its new surroundings. The surroundings have been superimposed on a nature which they fit but sorrily. Grace gives us the theological virtues. By these virtues we can know and love God, adhering to Him because of what He is in Himself. But these powers have been engrafted on a weak nature and they sit there uneasily. We can love God as He is in Himself, it is true, but our love has nothing of that spontaneity which characterizes the love of a child for the father who has given him life. We know Him and believe His word; but it is a word that falls on unresponsive ears and that gives a message far removed from what the heart holds dear. We may say that the theological virtues enable us to exist in the company of God, but they do not make us at home there. We feel that we have been lifted bodily out of the milieu into which we fitted so well and that now a voice rings in our ears whose accents are strangely cold, and a love rises in our hearts that fails to draw us in its wake. God is ours for the taking; but we have never been asked to do anything of the kind before, and our reaction is clumsy unrest.

In spite of the fact that what we have just described is an extreme case, it is undeniable that most souls will find that it is true to a certain degree of them also. They do not feel at home in the spiritual order. They know that it is far superior to nature, that the slightest spiritual joy is more intense and soul-satisfying than the most that earth can give; but this intellectual conviction has not become alive, has not become a part of self. The gift of grace is a stilt which raises them into precarious prominence, and they long for the homely feeling of the earth beneath their feet. Grace satisfies, perhaps, the purely rational in them; but the man—and, what is the same thing, the child—in them calls out for something to which it may cling, something warm, reassuring, familiar. Grace takes the child from his trains and soldiers and tells him to amuse himself with Him Who Is!

Can God have conceived no better plan than this for man?

CHAPTER II

THE SPIRIT BREATHETH

" . . . The Father Himself loveth you . . . " (John xvi. 27.)

The consideration of the suitability of man for adoption into God's family and for sharing in God's way of life has led us to the conclusion that if grace gave man nothing more than the new birth and the three theological virtues man would find himself at war with himself and not at peace with God. Yet if there is one fact clear in the whole of the revelation that God has made of Himself to us it is that He loves us and wishes us to be happy. How are these two positions to be reconciled?

God loves us. "For God so loved the world as to give His only begotten Son" (John iii. 16). The Incarnation and the Redemption are proof beyond all doubt that God loves the world. We cannot realize who God is and what the world is in relation to Him. No man would give his life for a thing he could make out of a block of wood. And yet the work of his hands has a value even when set against him who fashioned it. For it is made out of wood and wood it remains; the artist has just shaped it, and when the artist withdraws his hand the work endures, crystallized—if we may so speak—in the wood which is there altogether independently of his will and act. We do not find it quite so hard to imagine an artist dying for his work of art; but then the artist is a searcher after the beautiful, and his creation is rather a finding, and so he is, perhaps, ready to die for the worth of what he has found—for the truth and beauty he has

wrung from stone and canvas—rather than for the block
or the stuff in which he has revealed it. He dies then for
something greater than himself—for some refracted ray
from the throne of God.

God has not made us out of something else. There is
nothing in us but what God has put there. If a carpenter
makes a chair, it remains after he has gone, for the wood
was there before the carpenter and will remain when he
is no more, bearing in itself the imprint of his hand.
Were God ever to remove His hand from man, man would
cease to be. There was nothing there before God began
to work, and in which His work acquires permanency
when He withdraws His care. Before God uttered His
Fiat there was nothing. Were He ever to cease to utter
it what came from nothing would simply cease to be.

There is then nothing in man to attract God to him.
Moreover, God has all that must attract Him in
Himself.

God is the only being that does not need to go outside
itself to find happiness. God has in Himself the object
of every desire. We look for knowledge outside ourselves.
God finds wisdom in Himself; for He is the fount of
Wisdom. We love the goodness of the universe, but in
God's eyes it has only the goodness that He gives it. We
seek support in the friendship of powerful friends; God
is omnipotent and has no need of man. All that can be,
all that can be known, all that can be loved—all this
is in God, all this is God. God has the right and power
to live alone for all eternity in perfect bliss. And yet,
God made man and loved him.

God did not need man; God could get nothing from
man. Yet when man fell God so loved him as to come
on earth and die for him. Reason tells us of the solitary
God Whose life is knowing, Whose knowing is of self;

faith tells us of the gates of heaven thrown wide and of God Whose delight is to be with the children of men— of God who wept at the ingratitude of a faithless city. "O the depth of the riches of the wisdom and of the knowledge of God."

The God of the Christian is the God of faith and not the God of reason. No one can doubt that this God is the God of love, of tenderness, and mercy. He came down to man that man might be near to Him. His idea then of man—as raised by grace to intimacy with Him— is of a being who has returned to his home, a sinner received once more into his Father's house, and rejoicing in a Father's love. Yet this was hardly the idea we drew from our analysis of the nature of grace and of man whom it elevated. We had learned of one ill at ease, one lifted violently, as it were, out of his station and longing for the safe, if ignoble, repose of his earlier state. If there be any possibility of reconciling these apparently contra-dictory views it will be because God has so loved us as to have found a way of bridging the abyss between the Father and the adopted child.

Consider once more the case of the slum child adopted into a cultured family. The child is miserable. It does not know what to do. Its instincts seem to be all wrong. Its attempt to be at ease appears as forwardness; its timidity as sullenness. There is but one way of adapting the child to its new life. Let someone take it by the hand and guide it; guide it at every step, show it what to do, what to think, what to say. The child has the power to co-operate with this guidance, to assimilate the new modes of thought and feeling appropriate to its new life. This power it has from its rational nature. But it is in the child more a power of submitting to guidance than of finding the way. We all know the marvellous transforming power such kind and gentle leading has to remodel the mind of the child. The guide must be patient and loving. Time and again there will be a lesson to repeat, sulkiness and despondency to support. But the child will develop and the man will be worthy of the name he has acquired. It is the same thing that we need in the spiritual life. We have received from God a new nature and a new power of acting. But we need to be taught how to use them. Someone who knows the mind of God must take us by the hand and lead us step by step along His paths, put on our lips the words of thanks we should address to our Benefactor, rouse in us the feelings that should be ours when He draws nigh to us. Alone we are helpless. We know not what we should think, what we should ask for, how we should love. We need a guide who will live within our very souls.

There is a text of St Paul's which tells us the name of the guide of whom we speak. "For whosoever are led by the Spirit of God, they are the sons of God" (Rom. xiii. 14). It is the Holy Ghost who leads the adopted child of God. ". . . the things that are of God no man knoweth but the Spirit of God." The Holy Ghost knows the mind of God, knows how we should walk before the Lord, and so He Who is all love takes us by the hand and leads us. We know not what to say when God appears, "but the Spirit Himself asketh for us with unspeakable groanings" (Rom. viii. 26). We cannot love God as we should love Him. "The charity of God is poured forth in our hearts by the Holy Ghost" (Rom. v. 5). We find it hard to call Him Father. "You have received the spirit of adoption of sons whereby we cry: Abba (Father)" (Rom. viii. 15).

The Holy Ghost leads the child of God and does this through His gifts. It is in this power of submission to the divine guidance that the gifts consist essentially. But before considering them in detail it is well to draw attention to their more general characteristics.

The gifts of the Holy Ghost are what are known to the theologian and the philosopher as habits. The word has for them very much the same meaning as that given to it in ordinary usage. A habit means for the ordinary man a certain facility in doing something, resulting from repeated acts. For the theologian the operative habit is just such a facility, with however the proviso that it need not necessarily be acquired by repeated acts, but may have been poured into the soul directly by God Himself. In fact there are certain habits which give the power to perform acts so far above the possibilities of nature that we can have them only by infusion. To this group belong, among others, the theological virtues and the gifts of the Holy Ghost. Neither of these two classes of habits may be acquired by man's own unaided efforts: not the theological virtues, for they have as object God in Himself; nor the gifts of the Holy Ghost, for they are given us to fit us for the guidance proper to the state of adoptive children of God, and this state is one to which man cannot raise himself, but which comes as a gift from on high.

We mentioned in passing in the preceding paragraph that the gifts were operative habits. By this we mean that they are not just perfections of the substance of the soul, as is sanctifying grace, but that they reside in our faculties and give to them new power and vigour in the sense of a fuller responsiveness to the impulse of the Holy Ghost.

A second point to notice is that the gifts of the Holy Ghost are given to us to make us docile to the leading of the Holy Ghost. They are not given us as powers to be used as, and how, we will, but as powers of submitting ourselves readily to the guidance of one better and wiser than we. Of course our submission is not just passivity. We walk whither we are led, but we are none the less led by the fact that we walk.

Though reason can point to no example of a virtue which enables man to follow with docility the divine impulse, we all know of virtues whose whole function is to dispose a faculty to be guided by something higher than itself. The moral virtues are of this kind. They are perfections of the sensitive part and of the will by which both are subjected to the higher faculty of reason. Sense shrinks from a difficulty. Reason sees that there are things which should be done no matter how great the difficulty. And reason forces sense to advance and suffer, and by dint of continued forcing wears down the opposition of sense. Sense is drawn to pleasures which reason sees to be really harmful. So reason drags sense back, sense resisting the while; and after a time sense gets the habit of obeying at the first sound of the voice of reason, and even of anticipating its call. Now the Holy Ghost is the ultimate Arbiter of what is becoming in the spiritual life, just as reason rules the life of nature. Hence there must be something corresponding to the moral virtues in man by which he is disposed to follow the dictates of the Holy Ghost promptly and with ease, and this something is the gifts. Just as the moral virtues make the man to be fully reasonable, so the gifts make him to be the perfect child of God.

In submitting us in this peculiar way to the Holy Ghost the gifts add a divine element to our actions which they could not have otherwise. This is very clear if we take as example the knowledge of God given us by faith. We saw already that this knowledge bore the imprint of the strictly human in man. Man cannot see God and live. Faith does not enable him to see God but to believe in Him—to accept His word because it is His word. Reason knows through a multitude of concepts. It breaks up a truth into a number of fragmentary truths and the higher the truth the more numerous the fragments. Faith does the same thing. It tells us much about God and that in many words. God sees Himself in Himself, in one glance. That is the divine way of knowing God. Now, it is the peculiarity of the intellectual gifts, as we shall see later, that they give us a power of penetrating what faith reveals, and of unifying the body of truths it constitutes into a harmonious whole. That is to say, that they divinize faith. They make it like God's knowledge and not like that of man. In other words, the gifts raise our activity not merely to the level of God—for that is done by the theological virtues—but to the level of the way in which God acts. They enable us to live God's life in a way that is like God's way.

There is still one aspect of the gifts which should not be passed over in silence. It is that they make us more like to Our Lord. ". . . whosoever are led by the Spirit of God, they are the sons of God." Our Lord is the Son of God by nature and the Holy Ghost is His Spirit. We may say that the Holy Ghost was the mind of Our Lord. He always acted under the impulse of the Spirit. If He went into the desert, it was because the Spirit led Him there (Mark i. 12). It was in the Spirit that He drove out demons (Matt. xii. 28). Jesus applied to Himself the words of the prophet: "The Spirit of the Lord is upon Me, therefore He hath annointed me to preach the gospel to the poor" (Luke iv. 18). And it was the Holy Ghost Who presided at the greatest moment in the life of Our Saviour, when dying on the cross He offered Himself a pleasing sacrifice to the Father: "How

much more shall the blood of Christ Who by the Holy
Ghost offered Himself unspotted unto God, cleanse our
conscience from dead works to serve the living God"
(Heb. ix. 14).

The Holy Ghost was then the mind, the motive force,
in Christ. The Holy Ghost was the Spirit of the Son of
God. If we are to share in the sonship of Christ it can
only be by putting on Christ, by having in us the mind
of Christ. "We have the mind of Christ" (1 Cor. ii. 16).
We are the sons only if we act as did the Son of God,
and He acted as the Holy Spirit prompted Him. The
gifts are, then, the final perfection of our sonship. They
give to the sons to act as sons. They make us like Our
Lord, not indeed as a statue is like him whom it represents,
but as a younger brother often lives over again in himself
the thoughts, affections, and aspirations of an elder
brother whom he loves and looks up to. To be like Christ
is not a matter of putting on His dignity but of standing
in this world for what He stood for, of seeing the world
as He saw it, of hating what He hated, of loving what He
loved—all in and through His Spirit dwelling in us.

There are few truths more salutary than that the mind
of the Christian should be the Holy Ghost. We are prone
to think that grace is a kind of talisman, which if we but
have it on our person at any given moment, the dross
of any and every action becomes purest gold. Holiness
consists, we think, in getting as much grace as we can, and
then acting in perfect security under the impressions
of the world. I do not refer here to such impressions
as are manifestly sinful. What I have in mind are those
impressions which are those of any goodliving man who
has acquired the moral virtues. He is generous, hard-
working, just, affable. But all this springs from his
cultured paganism. He has not realised that the spring of

his activity should be outside himself, that there should
be a certain element of what I might call the unreasonable—or better, the "not-just-reasonable"—in all that
he does. There must be an element of the divine; for his
calling is to live with God as God lives with Himself.
We must be fools for Christ's sake (1 Cor. iv. 10). And
our folly must be that of the Apostles who after the first
Pentecost were put to scorn: "These men are full of new
wine" (Acts ii. 13). But they were full of the Holy Ghost
Who led them by the ways that the mind of man was too
short-sighted to fathom, too vulgar to respect. "And
it shall come to pass, in the last days (saith the Lord)
I will pour out of my Spirit upon all flesh: and your
sons and your daughters shall prophesy and your young
men shall see visions and your old men shall dream
dreams." Our Lord was the great seer of visions and
the great dreamer of dreams. He saw God and man
reunited on the wood of the Cross. He saw the Father
bending over His dying Son and gathering up into His
arms with Him the endless line of human sinners. He
dreamt of a Kingdom which was not of this world and of
grown men become little children. We shall see such
visions in the Spirit and in Him we shall dream such
dreams—but the world will know better and its pity
will be harder to bear than its hate. Happy shall we
be if we share in the "Is not this the carpenter's son?"
even though the sound of the "Crucify him" never burst
like music on our ears.

We see then that the final divinization of the soul is
the work of the gifts. The theological virtues enable
us to enter into contact with God as He really is in
Himself. But man if left to himself would use those
virtues in a human way. They are gifts too precious
to be subjected to man's clumsy, unsympathetic, handling.

They could miss their aim if used in man's way as opposed to God's way. We need to be taught God's way of using them; we need to be led in God's way of using them. Not merely the substance of the act must be divine; such must be its mode also. We must act the acts of God in the Spirit of God. We must act as the gifts enable us to act.

There seems to be no reason for hesitation in asserting in this connection that every single act which is specifically an act of a child of God proceeds from the gifts. The gifts are not for occasional use. The slum child commits a faux pas the moment it is left to itself. We cannot act as children of God unless the Holy Ghost be at our side. It is true that some of our good acts may be ungenerous—they may even appear to have just the minimum necessary to save them from being positively bad. Yet even such acts proceed from the gifts. The gifts have been hampered in their activity. They have seized us in an unruly moment and just managed to keep us straight. But they were there active, giving to our deeds that poor semblance of childlikeness they have managed to retain. God has not ceased to act when man is seen to resist—for to resist is to resist someone. The Spirit was there; else we could not have grieved Him.

CHAPTER III

THE GIFT OF UNDERSTANDING

"And the blind man said to him: Rabboni, that I may see."
(Mark x. 51.)

Before man could aspire to enter into the family of God
it was necessary to reveal to him that God was his Father,
and this message was central in all that Our Lord said
while He lived on earth. But it is one of the most striking
facts in the whole of the New Testament History that
this message, in itself so consoling, so much a fulfilment
of the noblest of human aspirations, fell upon deaf ears.
It need not be that men did not want to have God as
their Father. It may be that they wished Him to be a
Father of a kind other than His wisdom saw best. They
wished a Father Who would make them happy in this
life in their own petty way. They could not understand
a Father Whose range of vision would exceed their own.
And so there were but few who understood the message
of the Lord, and these few were of the little ones. "I
confess to thee, O Father, Lord of heaven and earth,
because thou hast hid these things from the wise and
prudent, and hast revealed them to little ones . . .
neither doth any one know the Father but the Son, and
he to whom it shall please the Son to reveal Him"
(Matt. xi. 27).

Our Lord's message to mankind was a secret torn from
the bosom of the Divinity. Man could see the sense of
the words in which it was expressed but its truth was
something he could not test. To accept it was possible

only through the gift of faith, the evidence of things that appear not. God's gift of Himself to man is entirely gratuitous. The gift of God and the power to accept the gift come from the same hand. The gift is the knowledge of God. The power of accepting is faith. But it is not sufficient to accept the gift of God. We feel a need of realizing the value of the gift. We feel the need of penetrating to the hidden sense of the word of Our Father—of not just saying: "It must be so since You said it," but of rising to: "I see what You mean and how wonderful it is!" Faith seeks vision. The word of God is not grasped till we have read it in the mind of God.

It is the gift of Understanding that gives us this power of penetrating the sense of the divine message, and we may see its need if we but press home still further the analogy of adoption by grace and human adoption which has been our guide so far. One of the first obstacles to be overcome in the newly adopted child is its incapacity to grasp the import of the information given it concerning the life into which it has been received. We speak here of a real incapacity which has nothing to do with bad will. The child is told that it has a new father and that he is good. It believes all this. It can repeat the formula and, if necessary, explain what it means. In addition, it really wishes to accept to the full a relationship which can only be beneficial to itself. One thing, however, is lacking. It has not read into the name of the father, the being who is all that it needs. It accepts the name and attributes it to the right individual, but it does not see that both name and individual are an answer to the void it feels within. It knows that it has a father, but it does not know fully what a father is. And so it is with any and every detail concerning its new life. The words are understood—they may even be familiar. But the idea is not penetrated. It lacks vividness, warmth, reality. And there always remains the suspicion that the whole thing is too good to be true and that the words may have some meaning other than that which appears on the surface. The child fears, and is unable, to make the intellectual plunge which its position demands.

The position of him who has been adopted into the family of God is still more difficult. God tells us the meaning of our new life in terms that are already familiar. He is a Father. Our Lord is a Brother. Our Lady is a Mother. He is good, merciful, forgiving: He wishes us to be happy. There is in all this no new word, and with Faith we can assent to the truth of every such statement. But we do not see in God all that we see in a Father though we know that it is really there. Even were we to go over in detail all the qualities of a Father and say to each one of these in turn: "I believe that my heavenly Father also has this property," the mind would not yet be at ease. There would be a sense of what one might term duress. All the light we should have about God would be thrown on Him from outside, forcing our assent, overpowering our reluctance to believe. But from the eyes of God Himself would shine no glance of understanding. He would stand out, cold, imposing, His mystery rendered all the more forbidding by the glare that throws it into such relief.

There is need then of a gift which will enable us to pass beyond the words of the message of faith and penetrate into its meaning. This gift is the gift of Understanding.

Understanding reveals to us the hidden meaning of the word of God in two ways: it cleanses our ideas from the accretions of sense; it enters into the heart of revelation.

An example of the cleansing power of Understanding may be seen in the tenth chapter of the Acts of the Apostles. There we read of the vision given to St Peter while he lived in the house of Simon. He saw as it were a linen sheet let down from heaven in which were all kinds of four-footed beasts and birds of the air and creeping things. And being hungry at the time he heard a voice saying to him: "Kill and eat". But he recoiled in horror from the idea of eating unclean food. Whereupon the voice spoke again telling him not to call unclean what the Lord had cleansed. And this vision appeared to him three times in all.

There appears to be no doubt but that Peter realized that the vision came from God. And the message it contained was one which the mind could grasp. It was merely to the effect that certain of the things he had been accustomed to regard as unclean in themselves were not so but had been cleansed by God. And still, though he could assent to the message, he could not grasp it. For we read that when the vision departed from him he doubted within himself what it should mean. Peter's mind was as yet in this matter the mind of a creature of the world. He could not look beneath the surface and see things with the eyes of God. Certain animals had always been regarded as unclean. And this uncleanness he thought to be inherent in the animals themselves. He had forgotten that God made all things good. He had perhaps never understood the fact that God made nothing for destruction, and that, *a fortiori*, He made no human being for destruction—and so when this message was revealed to him in terms which he regarded as unclean, his mind, obscured by a false idea of uncleanness, failed to penetrate its meaning, though he would have died sooner than deny its truth, whatever it might be.

This example, taken from the life of St Peter, is a somewhat extreme one. But it serves to show the real signification of what happens in our own lives. Let us take a truth to which everyone gives explicit assent: that we shall be happy with God for all eternity in heaven. Every Catholic will subscribe to that formula. But what does it mean for most of us? We have all our own ideas of happiness, gathered from daily life. The happiness we know comes from the company of friends. But the joy of heaven is not in the company of the friends we know, but of God Whom we do not know—Whom we know to be so unlike any earthly friend. We have experienced happiness the day we first had a home of our own, a place to rest our heads after the toil of the day and whence to regard the fever and the fret that pass the day. But heaven is not such a home. Heaven is immense. There we shall have no intimacy, no peace of retirement. To be in heaven is to be one of a multitude and to share in their life—to reveal one's life to them. Or again, we have tasted happiness when we did others good. But in heaven there are no needy souls, no possibilities of helping others. The life of heaven is a life of possessing, not of giving. And so it is that the happiness of heaven is a thing of which we have heard and in which we believe, but of which we know nothing with that deep security and reassuring vision that alone quiet the anxious mind. Our idea of happiness is too earthly. It is wide enough to embrace the happiness of heaven, but too bound up with earth to let the soul see clear.

And then one day the Holy Ghost speaks to our souls. We think of God and we think of happiness, and like a wave joy surges in our hearts as we feel for the first time in our lives that man can be happy with God. Were we asked to explain this new state we could say nothing that could not have been said before. Now, as then, we believe that happiness is the lot of the saints in glory. But happiness as a spiritual experience has dawned upon the mind, a happiness which is not of this world, but which still is happiness; a happiness which we can define only in familiar words that now mean what they never meant before. This is the mystery of the gift of Understanding. It gives no new ideas, no new words, no new formulae. It is just a power of reading the open page of revelation, of seeing something of what was the mind of God when He spoke through the human lips of His Son.

Understanding is not then a kind of beatific vision in which the mind reads God's message as it is in the mind of God. It is just a power of grasping the import of the message as it stands revealed in the treasury of the Church. But it is a gift. The unaided mind cannot accept the word of God; without Understanding we cannot lay its meaning bare. Understanding is the perfection of faith. Our Lord showed the need of His gift when He appeared to His disciples after His resurrection. Hitherto they had heard His word and accepted it. But He saw that there was still something to be accomplished in them; and so "He opened their understanding that they might understand the scriptures" (Luke xxii. 45).

It will not be irrelevant to indicate certain of the cases in which we stand in need of the gift of Understanding. The general principle laid down earlier in the chapter was that Understanding purifies the idea from the obscurity of sense imagery and so enables us to see the true meaning of revelation. There will then be need of the gift in as many ways as there are ways in which a spiritual truth may be hidden or obscured. It would be impossible to enumerate all these ways in full detail. The following are some of the more obvious.

A spiritual reality may be hidden in a thing of sense which is its cause. In this way grace is contained in the sacraments. We know, on the word of God, that the sacraments confer grace. But the eye sees only a material object and the ear hears only a human voice. God is working there in that voice and in that thing. His grace is given through the sacrament. But it is only the Holy Spirit Who can teach us to see in the visible sign the instrument of the Most High and nothing else—it is only He Who can divest the thing of sense of every element except the fact of its being the tool of Our Redeemer. Faith tells us that it is His tool in very truth; but only Understanding will make it be present to the mind under this aspect to the exclusion of every other.

Again it may be question of a truth contained in a parable of Our Lord or in some event of our lives. The parables were meant for our instruction. But some there are who fail altogether to see their lesson. Our Lord has told us that the kingdom of heaven is like a grain of mustard seed. We know that He means to tell us by that, that the beginnings of our spiritual life are weak, but that, in time, grace throws out deep roots and grows into a mighty tree. Yet we have no real, living perception of how small a thing the germ of grace can be in us nor of what it may grow into. We are like people who have heard how the sound of a voice is sufficient to set an avalanche in movement and have done their best to bring the idea home to themselves and then, one day, they experience the reality, and they see that their manufactured concepts fell infinitely short of its overpowering majesty. There will come a day when the Holy Ghost will give us not only to hear, but to see, that the kingdom of heaven is a mustard seed. And in that day what we had known before will seem as trash.

The events of our lives are also so many parables. There is a lesson hidden in much of what appears trivial or ordinary. The goodness of God to us is often hidden in happenings that at first sight seem unpleasant. We may have looked forward to some holiday; and then when it comes the weather is bad and we can do nothing. God has arranged all this. But without the gift of Understanding we cannot see that His care for us was at the back of the apparent disappointment. For we might have been led into sin, or met people whose friendship would draw us no nearer to God; or just simply have arrived at the stage when we should think that after all the world had a lot to be said for it and could give more real pleasure than God would have us think—and God, Who cares for each of us as if there were no others, spoiled the holiday to save or enrich our souls.

We have already insisted on the necessity of the gift of Understanding to enable us to get out of revelation all that is in it. It is a well-known fact that certain souls are capable of drawing lesson after lesson from what was apparently the simplest of texts. We all know how St Theresa of the Child Jesus deepened her spirituality by reading: "Give to him that asketh of thee, and from him that would borrow of thee turn not away" (Matt. v. 42). The text appears on the surface to be easy enough. It recommends us not to be overharsh with those needy ones who turn to us for assistance. And yet St Theresa, enlightened by the Holy Ghost, read in it the Cross— complete and selfless subjection to the cross that others press upon our shoulders. If it be true of so many that they can read page after page of Holy Scripture and find there nothing that they do not know already, or that is not more attractively said in books of popular spirituality, does this not point to the fact that they try to read with their own little minds and in the light of man-given principles? The truths of God are to be read in the light of the Holy Spirit; and those who read in this light read not in darkness. Their moments of scripture-reading are no longer painful toiling in a waste and barren land, but every word they read becomes in them a fountain of water springing up to life everlasting.

We might mention in the last place that it is the gift of Understanding which enables us to enter with relish into the great feasts and devotions of the Church. The doctrine of the Immaculate Conception was opposed by theologians who were by no means the least able or the least pious in the history of the Church; yet the simple faithful, under the guidance of the Holy Ghost, saw that it was true. And even when a doctrine has been officially promulgated there always remain certain souls who, while they do not deny the truths of the dogma, believe that they can get on quite well without integrating it into their lives. It is of course a fact that it is by no means necessary to find a place in one's spiritual outlook for each individual devotion that finds adherents among the faithful. But there are certain devotions which are of primary importance and which must be understood at the price of remaining spiritually undeveloped without them.

A strong personal devotion to Our Lord is of such a kind. And yet reason will tell us that the Father seeks such as adore Him in spirit and in truth, and that it is only by freeing ourselves from attachment to the Sacred Humanity that we can be united to the divinity. Or

again it may tell us that Our Lord came on earth to draw
us to the Father and that provided we are drawn to the
Father it does not make much difference whether we
think of the Son or not. All these appeals to a greater
spiritualization of Christianity are vicious. But they can
be backed by plausible reasons—so plausible indeed that
there are spiritual people who try to live without the
human note of this essential devotion to Our Saviour.
They admit, of course, a well-bred and gentlemanly
sense of gratitude to the God-man Who died to redeem
them; but they consider that it is in the best interests of
both parties to transact all spiritual business directly
with the Father.

Even good souls may have some such difficulty as
this in their relations with Our Lord. They may find it
hard to fit Him in practice into their lives even though
they be tolerably well instructed in the theology of the
Incarnation. Their defect is that they have not as yet
understood the Incarnate Word in the light of the gift
of Understanding. The knowledge of Our Lord must
be lived, experienced knowledge—not a matter of
question and answer, of premise and conclusion. St
Thomas thought he knew Our Lord until he received the
invitation to put his hands into His pierced side and into
the Most Precious Wounds of His Hands. And then
he could only cry out: "My Lord and my God". He had
now come to live the mystery of Jesus. His Lord and
Saviour was not just the sum of certain qualities. He was
a living value, an answer in flesh and blood to the riddle
of life, Life Itself Incarnate and gazing into the once
doubting eyes of Thomas.

Devotion to Our Lady is also the fruit of the gift of
Understanding. No amount of reasoning will ever
convince a man that he is spiritually incomplete unless

he be devout to the Mother of God—who, though full of grace, is but a creature. Not until the Holy Ghost reveals to him what it is to have a mother in the spiritual order will he be devout to Our Lady. It is in vain that he will meditate on the fragility of human nature, our need of a protectress, the dignity of her who was chosen by God to be His mother—all this is but the spade work that prepares the soil of the mind. The idea of Mary comes from the Holy Ghost. It is He Who shows us the real living and loving person hidden beneath the traditional formulae. We come to know Our Lady as we come to know any other person—through intimate contact. And this spiritual contact is possible only to him who sees Mary with the eye of Understanding. For her brightness dazzles reason's eye and makes her mystery all the more baffling.

To the gift of Understanding is opposed the vice of spiritual dullness or stupidity. In the purely natural order we find a kind of understanding which consists in quickness of perception, intellectual alertness. Opposed to this is a heaviness, sluggishness, intellectual blindness. The same phenomena are observed in the spiritual order as well. The gift of Understanding makes us spiritually keen and wide-awake; its absence makes of the spiritual a sealed book. If a person finds that his mind is incapable of grasping spiritual realities—not, of course, in a speculative way, or in so far as they are part of the science of theology, but in so far as they are necessary for the direction of his life—he should, it is understood, see if this may not be due to lack of instruction, lack of familiarity with the terms God uses in speaking with us; but he will most likely find that it is due to the fact that his life is not under the guidance of the Holy Ghost. It is the Holy Ghost Who lights up our darkness, placing at every danger point the beacon of the word of God, strengthening our feet with the vigour of His grace.

Still more pernicious to the soul than mere blindness or weakness of vision is that terrible perversion of mind by which all that we see is defiled by the spirit of this world and the spirit of darkness. A life of sin—and particularly a life of the sins of sense—warps the mind to the extent of making it, of itself, unfit to receive any impressions other than those of the senses. Where the pure see God, the impure see sin and the invitation to sin. There is, of course, a temperamental peculiarity which colours, in certain people, all thoughts and images with an appeal to passion. This appeal is not incompatible with the gift of Understanding. For, as we have just said, Understanding effects a practical, not speculative, purification of the mind, causing it to see in all that it sees an *effective* invitation to the love of God. And the person tried by temptation, but still resisting, has in fact received this effective invitation and is resisting under its influence. It is to a practical, effective, sense-colouring, that we refer now—from one that proceeds from the desire to sin, and which finds fuel in the most innocent thought or image. And the state of mind from which this proceeds is the product of the spirit of darkness. This perversity is his gift. Put yourself under his sway and he will enable you to blind yourself to the danger of your position. That is the reward he has promised to his faithful ones—to those who have defiled their hearts.

Our Lord has addressed one word to those whom the world and Satan have blinded. "Blessed are the pure of heart for they shall see God."

CHAPTER IV

THE GIFTS OF KNOWLEDGE
AND WISDOM

"The things that were gain to me the same I have counted
loss for Christ." (Phil. iii. 7.)

The soul that has the gift of Understanding has received
the power of penetrating the mind of God. There remains
yet one step to be taken: knowing the mind of God the
soul must now judge the world in terms of divine values.
This is the work of the gifts of Knowledge and Wisdom.

Our little adopted vagrant has learned to know his
father's voice and to grasp its message. His new life,
however, is not intended to be purely passive. He must
learn, it is true; but having learned he must set himself
to regulate his thoughts and deeds in accordance with
the new principles so learned. He must view events
as his father would view them. He must be able to
sense what would be his father's opinion in matters in
which for some reason or other he cannot be consulted.
Until the time arrives when his own spontaneous judg-
ments will be those of his father there will always be
a sense of strain, a sense of the uncongenial, in his life.
He is perfectly at home only when life is as he feels it
should be, and when in the face of every difficulty or
crisis he feels that his course of action is clear, and,
what is more, is inevitable and reasonable.

God's children—and we are all, young and old,
nothing more, nothing less, than that—experience the
same need. Unless we are in possession of a body of

principles in virtue of which we can regulate thought and action we live in an atmosphere of strain. The least that will happen to us is the fear of the unexpected, the uneasy danger of being confronted by the unknown. The man who feels that his intellectual stock-in-trade is equal to the task of classifying any problem likely to arise goes about his task with assurance. The half-equipped, painfully conscious of the chinks in his armour, never plunges fully into the fray of life and so never emerges victor.

The world has its knowledge and its wisdom—folly though they be in the eyes of God. It is no uncommon experience to meet a man who views life consistently from a favourite angle, never doubting the validity of his categories and the absurdity of all that refuses to fit into them. It is the possession of this knowledge and false wisdom that produces obstinacy in all its forms, from the weak, but willed, indecision of the moral coward to the harsh brutality of him who rules his fellows from the imagined height of his ripe experience. The coward who fears to venture takes refuge in some favourite maxim. He relies on the view that hurry prevents speed or that a bird in the hand is worth two as yet winging their way heavenwards, to justify his childish inaction. He has a principle and judges thereby. He feels safe while he hangs on to his principle; it gives him a grip on life; it affords an unfailing method of approach to the unknown. But as he grasps it, the principle is false and his wisdom petty. He thinks he rules life; but he buys a chimerical victory by never risking a defeat.

Still more despicable than the coward—for the coward scarcely gets even the illusion of joy in life—is the cock-sure. One need not be very old to be cock-sure. The particular form of the vice I have now in mind is found in young as well as old, and this in spite of the fact that it arises from and relies upon a supposedly wide experience. There are people whose minds are so penetrating—in their own opinions, of course—that a very short time suffices to give them the key to the riddle of life. After a few choice experiments they know what everything is about. They arrive at this happy state by a radical process of simplification. For they reduce all the main problems of life to one or two, and then answer them. Thus, there are people who reduce life to what concerns themselves alone and their dealings with others. It may happen that in matters that concern themselves alone they do not make much difficulty for the rest of mankind. Thus, it might be possible to enjoy a social evening in the company of a man of this type. But in all that concerns meeting others as man to man he will prove a brute. For experience has taught him that men are essentially dishonest. No appeal of starving poverty will ever move him, for he knows that the poor have no higher aim in life than to earn their bread by telling lies. It never strikes him that it is good for him to allow himself, occasionally at least, to be deceived by frauds, rather than to turn hungry members of Christ Crucified away from his door in mistake. He has his principle and will apply it though to do so is to tear flesh from bone. He has been taught by experience and is too wise now to be deceived again.

The spiritual man has his principles too, and his life is shaped by them. In a wonderful passage in that most beautiful of epistles—the Epistle to the Hebrews—St Paul reveals one of the many Christian ways of viewing things: "For we have not here a lasting city, but seek one that is to come" (Heb. xiii. 14). Life is but the way to something higher—to a more noble life which is hid with

Christ in God; all that is in the world and the world itself will pass away, and we shall be unmoved at its decay, for we have set our hearts on something higher. We have been deceived by friends, by those very friends in whom we thought we could have trusted even unto death. Their ingratitude will hurt. But must we fall beneath the blow? Rather let us rise, more full than ever of confidence in the worth of life; for our real treasure is untouched, our real strength has not been impaired. We had hoped to serve God by promoting some particular work that seemed so necessary, and it has failed. Why should we fret? God's work is one—the building of the heavenly Jerusalem; and that is a city built with human tears and not with human hands. Though the world seem to crumble and threaten to entomb us in its dust, we have within us the power to rise above the ruins, for do we not know that its decay is no more real than its glory, and that our feet tread even now the streets of a holy city ". . . that hath foundations; whose builder and maker is God" (Heb. xi. 10).

Any truth of the spiritual order may be used as a vantage point to survey the world. There are souls who find that difficulties vanish if they be considered in relation to grace. Such souls evaluate things in terms of their influence upon grace vivifying their souls. They are willing to pluck out an eye if its presence be harmful to the life of grace within them (Matt. v. 29). Others find their fulcrum in the essential nothingness of the world (cf. Matt. xvi. 26) and use this fulcrum to remove every obstacle that strews their way. Others again may find an irresistible appeal in some virtue—in humility, or chastity, or brotherly love—and by resolving every demand conscience makes into an opportunity for the exercise of the virtue they hold so dear, find strength to do the hardest tasks and to bear the most irksome burdens. And in all these cases it is a matter of reducing life to a controllable unity. For though it be true that the best way to attack difficulties is to approach them one by one, they must be approached each time in the strength and the spirit that has given the first victory. When this is the case each new struggle is rather a promise of victory than a threat of defeat. Man faces life as the child of the All-Powerful.

We have been speaking so far of the gift of Knowledge. This gift is a power of judging or evaluating things in terms of created spiritual realities. By created spiritual realities are meant grace, the human soul, the sacraments, and all supernatural things which are not God. The gift enables us to see the world and all that is in it in relation to them. No matter what happens to us, no matter what intellectual problem presents itself, it will be considered as worthy of consideration to the extent to which it has supernatural worth. As was said in connection with the gift of Understanding, the knowing and judging which come up for consideration here are not just speculative. They are before all else practical and effective. The gifts do not necessarily give new information which, considered as mere information, could not have been obtained otherwise. They give what we might call affectively-coloured information; that is to say, they give information which inflames heart and will and which under this affective (and consequently effective) aspect cannot be obtained by any enquiry whatever. The gift of Knowledge then is not just a power of judging things in their relation to certain spiritual matters, it is a power of judging which sets the will aflame. When, under the action of the Holy Ghost, acting in us through the gift of Knowledge, we see that a certain matter is a danger to our soul, we do not stop at the judgment, but conceive at once hatred of the evil and the will to flee it. For the Holy Ghost is concerned more with our salvation than with our intellectual education. He enlightens us in order to lead us to God, and the surest test of the provenance of an idea is its godwardness or its sterility.

St Thomas Aquinas points out very beautifully that the gift of Knowledge leads to the beatitude: "Blessed are they that weep." Knowledge is concerned mainly, as we have said, with created things. If ever it considers God it does so in so far as He is Author of the created, its Sanctifier, or its End. But the created as such is that which can draw man away from God. And so we see in the created rather cause for regret—for sorrow for past infidelities—than for joy.

And indeed one of the most common forms of Knowledge is that based upon the perception of the transitoriness of the world and its nothingness in comparison with the value of one soul. This is the knowledge Our Lord Himself recommended to us when He asked what it would profit man to gain the whole world while suffering the loss of his soul; and it was the same knowledge that the Apostle taught when he spoke of earth as no lasting city. The created can lead us to God only by losing itself in God. We find God in creatures only if we seek Him alone in them. And so, to turn to God through the created is to tear oneself from all in the created that is not God, to sacrifice the beauty that will pass for that beauty which is ever old and ever new. To possess God is joy unending. To lose what seems fair is to weep. But blessed are they that mourn for they shall be comforted in the possession of their God. Though they have not here a lasting city, they are already children of God and members of His household, and their weeping is already turned into joy. For it is a weeping that springs from and leads to love. Through our tears, as in no other way, do we see the Father Who has begotten us.

The blessedness of our mourning is in the promise it bears of comfort, and in the same way the gift of Knowledge points necessarily to something higher still, the gift of Wisdom. We mourn at the loss of the world and are comforted in the possession of God; we judge through created eyes and weep; we judge through the eyes of God and we find peace. Over and above the created, supernatural though it be, is God Himself, and the gift which enables us to view the world in its relation to God Himself is the gift of Wisdom.

We saw that the world has its knowledge. It has its wisdom as well. This time let us consider a wisdom which is not evil but which is just natural. In every walk of life there is some one master idea which is the key to all its problems. The great soldier is not the man who has filled his head with facts and figures and nothing else; he is rather the man who has an ordered grasp of all the facts and figures connected with his calling. Factual information is necessary; but mastery of a subject comes from a grasp of its basic principle. Once this principle is mastered the difficult problems fall naturally into their place. What appears chaos to the uninitiated is order to him who knows the secret of its order, and knowing this secret he can impose himself where others draw back impotently.

The man who has seized the master-idea which unlocks the world's secret is said to be wise; he has the quality of wisdom. What wisdom is on the purely natural level is a rather difficult question to answer. A philosopher would say that it consists in the grasp of the essential distinction between potency and act, so that the wise man, in the highest sense of the term, is he who distinguishes in every problem the place that must be given to potency and the place due to act, and resolves the problem along the general lines which he knows to be valid from his preliminary study of these two basic ideas. No matter what it may be that invites his study, it must be either potency or act or a mixture of both and so cannot escape the two categories which constitute his ultimate line of defence against the onslaught whether of ego or non-ego. It is unnecessary to insist on the moral sterility of these categories. They afford a speculative solution of the widest generality to any possible question, but the very generality of the solution makes its appeal to the will feeble. The will is drawn to the concrete existing good, not to the universal idea; and the philosopher will often find himself willing and doing the potency that his intellect declares so inferior to the insipid act.

In the spiritual order there is, however, a master idea which gives a solution at once speculative and practical to the riddle of life. That idea is the idea of God. Judge things from God's angle and you see their true meaning; what is still more, you judge them from the angle of Him Who made them and in the hollow of Whose hand they are. God is the source of all that is, and it is He Who has given it its meaning. God dominates the universe, grasps it in one idea, rules it in one act. The universe can neither be dominated, nor grasped, nor ruled, in any real and lasting way unless by entering into the mind and power of God. To him who stands outside God the universe is an enemy, an opposing force which at any moment may gain the upper hand and crush him whom it defeats. To him who views it from God's point of view, through the eyes of God, it is but an instrument, the faithful doer of a master's bidding, terrible only to him who does not know it.

Man needs to master the world even in thought. Man is but a puny being. There is not a single man to whom this has not been brought home time after time, especially in the presence of some one of those great crises of death or sickness when tears are our only solace, and to cry is to admit defeat. Wisdom is the mastery of the world —the reduction of its chaos to an ordered unity which we have understood; the reduction of the unknown and the unfamiliar to the oft-experienced and the loved. It is giving life a meaning and finding in its meaning peace.

The truly wise is he who judges things from the point of view of God. A calamity is really such, only if God's interests are damaged—and even then we are at peace, for we know that God's will will infallibly be done, that He has plans of which we know nothing. The world seems to hate us; we have no friends; those on whom we depended have turned away. But we have a Father in Heaven Whose most pressing advances are heard when others desert us. God is always there, and He is a Father, and a Father cannot allow harm to come to His children. We have need of but confidence and love. God will look after the rest. And this is our great wisdom—to know that there is Someone Who cares and watches, and that He is both good and powerful.

Our wisdom then is but a simple thing. But there is no problem that it does not resolve. God is the centre of the universe and it can have no surer support. But we must notice that it is above all else an affective wisdom. It is not theoretical. It is a reduction of all to God known more in love than in thought. Faith tells Who God is and what He does in the world. But faith does not see God nor does it taste that the Lord is sweet. And it is more this sweetness of the Most High that is meant when we speak of Him as a Father than any mere intellectual idea. We love God; God is an Object that the will feels to be all Goodness, and so we trust in Him, know that all that He does and permits is for the best, know that there are in Him treasures of wisdom and knowledge that we can never grasp—all this is what we mean when we call God a Father. For the child, the father—or more commonly the mother—is just a matter of someone loved. The child can give no reasoned analysis of the qualities its mother has which make her so dear. It is only when the child flies to its mother's arms and clasping her tight is penetrated by her warm living reality that it really experiences motherhood. And this experience is a feeling, a matter of love. We know God only when we love Him, when we live in His embrace. For the soul that lives in the embrace of God there are no problems. She has experienced God in love and found in Him the answer to every enquiry, the goal of every quest. God is my Father and a Father is one Whom I can love and trust: this is the practical key to life. With this reply ever on our lips we shall hardly be reputed learned or deep; we shall merely be able to face up to life. The Holy Ghost is not given us to teach us how to write books, but to help us to live well.

It should not appear strange to us that Wisdom is, to a great extent, a matter of love. Man, the whole integral man, is not just an intellect; he is will and feeling as well. No man can rise above the storms of life and withstand unshaken the assaults of time, who relies on only one of these three great forces. The intellect enlightens, but it does not enkindle. Feeling enkindles, but it is blind and vacillating. The will is strong but blind and cold. And the work of living demands light, strength, and warmth. There are people who have clear ideas on their duty to their country; but their hearts remaining cold, they serve in the cause of self. There are others all enthusiasm for their country's good, but whose misguided efforts work its ruin. And there are others again, who in sheer dogged earnestness, crush out opposition in the service of an unworthy cause. None of these are men in the full sense of the term, none of these are really equipped for life. Their armoury is too specialized for the manysidedness of life.

In the spiritual order, feeling and love are one. Hence the complete man is he who knows and loves; not just he who knows nor he who loves, but he whose knowledge leads to and is fed by love. Knowledge of the right does not exclude love of evil. In fact, sin would be impossible were there not a certain knowledge of the right. On the other hand, however, there can be no true love without knowledge. There may be the appearance of the love of God—but it is love of a false god, a love possibly of self. To be fixed immovably in God man must adhere to Him by both intellect and will. If the world is to find no grip on man it must be because every fibre of his being has been seized by God. And spiritual knowledge grows on love. Faith sees God in the created word of revelation. Love penetrates unto the very Godhead. There are no recesses of the divinity to which love does not gain entry. Love is love of God as He will be loved when the revelation of eternity will dispel the veil of faith. There are no secrets for love; love has searched out the hidden things of God. And hence it is that our poor ideas of God acquire life and vividness in love. Love has preceded vision and so must perfect our faith.

A point somewhat slurred over in the sections dealing with Understanding and Knowledge, may now be clear, namely the source of the new intellectual vigour given in the gifts of the Holy Ghost. It is, of course, evident that the Holy Ghost is its source. But there is one of the theological virtues which He uses to produce in us His gifts and that virtue is charity. By charity, or love, we are attuned to God. Just as no one can read the mind of a man better than someone who loves him, so love is the door to the mind of God. A wife standing at the bedside of a dying husband will know what every half-formed word, what every half-stifled sigh, is meant to communicate. The reason is that she loves. A mother knows, no one better, what her child's whispered message means, for love enables her to feel with it. Love of God enables us to feel with God, and so to decipher what to others appears chaos. We read the hidden meaning of His word, for we feel what He felt when he spoke to us. We judge the world in terms of the spiritual things He made, for we are drawn to them as like to like. We know His own eternal majesty because we have loved it. "And he that loveth me shall be loved of my father: And I will love him and will manifest myself to him" (John xiv. 21). The Lord is manifest to them that love Him.

The defect of wisdom may be termed stupidity. It is of two kinds, according as it implies absolute incapacity to judge things in the light of spiritual principles or just a certain difficulty in doing so. Even in the natural order there are stupid people who grasp all matters indifferently from the wrong angle and others who are just slow to see things in their true light and never arrive at a really thorough knowledge of them. But the most dangerous form of the vice is that which springs from indifference to and distaste for God. Wisdom is called "sapientia" in Latin as it is a knowledge springing from a relish of its object. Where there is no such relish, but rather a positive distaste, there can be no "sapientia." Instead there is disgust for the things of God, intense weariness in His presence. The fool, we are told, said there is no God. But the man who is weary of God is worse than the fool. For he sees God everywhere. He cannot but refer life to God. God looms large on his horizons and he does not want God. He lives in the inescapable presence of God and every instant is death. God seems to dog his footsteps, to watch and spy his every thought, and for him to rebel beneath His yoke makes it but cut deeper into the soul.

There are, thank God, but few souls who have this vice. Those that have are they who hate God and judge His works with lips that blaspheme. None are more miserable than they. They have nothing to oppose to the forces they feel ranged against them but their own impotent hate. They know that victory cannot be theirs, that they are really defenceless, that their bravado is petty folly. But hate is stronger than reason. There is but one thing that can conquer hate and that is love. They, however, have turned their backs on love, and empty hate is their portion. How great is the folly that can make life a hell and eternity a damnation.

The Holy Ghost will give us the Wisdom we need. He who is all love will teach us to see the Father in love and so will make us wise. But our wisdom will be but the wisdom of little children. For love is folly to those who resist its charm.

CHAPTER V

THE GIFT OF FORTITUDE

"Why are you fearful, O ye of little faith." (Matt. viii. 26.)

Perfection arises from the presence of all the principles that constitute a thing. The absence of even one is sufficient to reduce perfection to imperfection. The perfect man is the man who has within him all that is needed for the great adventure of life. One defect in his equipment eliminates him at once from the ranks of those who experience life to the full. We have seen already that the spiritual man needs the intellectual equipment of three gifts. We shall see in the following chapter that one more intellectual gift is needed as well. But even with this latter man has not all of which he stands in need. For he has appetition as well as intellect, and he reaches the goal of life by the aid of every power that is in him. Even sense must be enlisted in the service of his supernatural striving. Sense will need to be purified, to be disciplined, to be shorn of all in it that is merely sense. But it cannot be ignored. It is an element in the make up of man, and he can give of the best that is in him only if sense be regarded unequivocally as an inveterate enemy or a possible friend. It cannot be left aside as of no account.

The intellect will point out the goal of our endeavour and the paths that lead thereto. The goal will be God Our Father; the path will be the life of spiritual childhood. But the goal must be reached and the paths trodden, and here one has need of courage. Be an ideal as noble as it may be, the cowardly will turns guiltily aside at the prospect of the effort its attainment must cost. Without the intellect no horizons open themselves invitingly to human eyes, and without a courageous will the surrounding waste keeps the soul confined within its own narrow bounds. Everything that is worth having costs. There is need of unremitting effort, need of bearing opposition from without and cowardly groanings from within. The life of man is a warfare in which there can be no non-combatants. He who hesitates to draw on all his resources is lost; and he who sees where victory lies but hesitates to make the move upon which all—even the possibility of safe retreat—depends, will perish in the danger he could have overcome.

This truth—that courage is essential in the spiritual life—is especially apparent if we consider the fact that the soul in the state of grace is an adopted child of God. An adopted child has need of courage, and of a courage of a higher kind than it had before. Before adoption the problems it had to face were those of a slum child, and it brought to bear upon them all the resources of courage and tenacity found in such children. It needed but little to keep body and soul together and knew no greater difficulty than that (but how difficult it must have been at times!) of fighting for the daily bread, of waiting when it did not come. The difficulties of its new life are of an entirely different order. It is expected to take a certain place in society; perhaps to go to a school where its antecedents will inevitably be known and there will be petty persecution to support. Later on there will be a business to direct, responsibilities to face. For nothing of all this was it prepared by upbringing. Its courage will stand it in but poor stead in the face of such problems. It has courage—but not the right kind of courage. It can face problems—but not the problems that it is now asked to face. And then there is the difficulty of the new life itself, independently of the social relations it sets up. Will the child be able to sustain the effort of restraint, of self-repression, of application to study? Does it not appear that the whole adoption is doomed to failure, not this time because of the defective outlook of the child, but because of the impossible demands made upon its courage?

To wage the new battle the child needs new strength. It must face up to its social obligations not in the power that it has by birth, but in the power that it has by adoption. A man as individual can do but little. In an official capacity, however—if he be, for example, a policeman—he acts relying not on himself but on that of which he is representative. The policeman is the representative of law and right, and what he does has all the dignity and inviolability attached to law and right. The child must face his fellows not because of what it was but because of what it has become. It stands in the presence of others invested with all the authority of its new father. Whoever harms it harms a powerful and influential family. Whatever it does in the name of that family has in the eyes of the world the same value that it would have were it the act of the head of the family himself. Even in what concerns life in the bosom of the family the child has not to struggle against unequal odds. The life to which it has been admitted is new, but there are opportunities at hand of adapting itself to it; the family is able and willing to provide the necessary education; there will be no difficulty in providing capable and devoted teachers; books can be had for the purchasing; lessons in deportment are not hard to obtain; faults of grammar may be corrected; in fact,

there is no obstacle to success which may not be overcome through the means at the family's disposal if only
the child has sufficient intelligence and good will to
employ them. And so the child faces life bravely, with
confidence; for though the battlefield be a strange one
there are allies who know its every twist and turn.
It gains courage by relying on people stronger and wiser
than itself.

The spiritual life also is one that calls for the exercise
of courage. It has reached its perfection only when self
is dead, and there is nothing that calls for greater courage
than to be one's own executioner in the spiritual sense
of the term. It means giving up everything to which one
might cling for support and abandoning self entirely and
without reserve to God. It is not so difficult to fight when
the enemy is outside oneself. For though he be strong—
though he even succeed in overpowering us—there is
always an inner castle of intellect and will to which he
has no entry, and we enter the conflict knowing that all
cannot be lost. This secret fortress will remain in our
possession to the very end. Our humanity, our personality, our worth in our own eyes—all these are ours no
matter how crushing the defeat. They may be moment-
arily obscured. The magnitude of our losses may distract
us for a moment from the treasure that has been salvaged
—but this is only for a time, for the ego has the vital
urge and refuses to bend for ever beneath the yoke.

Someone may feel tempted to object that the fiercest
struggles are not necessarily those fought out in the
interior of a man's soul. Have there not been cases of
men whose whole existence has been embittered by
financial loss, or treachery of friends, or some other
encounter with the world outside them from which they
emerged defeated and crushed? Do not such cases seem

to disprove the contention that it is the struggle with self that is the acid test of courage?

Far from being exceptions such instances prove our contention. The ultimate cause of defeat is not the set-back that has resulted from the encounter with the outside world but the devaluation of his own personality in the eyes of the person who has suffered the set-back. It was the interior crisis that proved his undoing, not the mere loss of money or friends. The man who has faith in himself and in his power to survive for what he is worth in himself cannot be crushed by any disaster that leaves self intact. If he falls it will be because he has lost confidence in the value of his own personality. The exterior conflict occasions an interior one and it is this latter that proves his ruin.

Suicide is no answer to the threat of moral defeat either. The man who dies voluntarily and wittingly by his own hand is a coward. He fears to risk his personality in the struggle of life. The danger that threatens is great. To it he can oppose only his manhood. And he prefers to take refuge in escape into what he persuades himself is the unknown rather than to appear before the world as a man and nothing more—shorn of all the frumpery that makes a man look like a god, reduced to plain John Jones with nothing to commend him to himself or to his fellows beyond the fact that he was born a child of Adam and has a soul that can be saved.

Now it is precisely this fear which leads moral cowards to suicide that is the most fundamental of those that lie in waiting for the child of God. If we wish to deal with God we must regard Him as God and ourselves as what we really are and nothing else. We must divest ourselves of the idea that circumstances of birth make us more attractive in God's eyes. We have, in other words, to

live in the presence of God without one single piece of
that armour we find so useful when we come into contact
with our fellow men. We need to realize that money
does not count in God's eyes. Other people may be
influenced or beaten down by money. God must be influenced if we are to be saved, but money will never
influence Him. We may have a good reputation, as
scholarly, or gifted, or even just entertaining, and such
a reputation will open many doors and surmount many
a difficulty. God is more learned and scholarly than we
and He does not need to be entertained; and so one more
weapon falls from our grasp. Where then can we turn?
Does not the ego remain? the indomitable spirit? that
which makes a man master of his fate and captain of
his soul? Is there not the fact that I am somebody,
and hence count, even if weighed against God? This
is the last entrenchment of the soul that tries to go to
God by a way other than God Himself, and it is one that
first falls perhaps with death, but is in a state of siege
as long as life is lived sincerely, for we must bring ourselves to realize that the self counts for nothing as opposed
to God. The self is of value. It was for selves that God
died upon the Cross. But it was because of the divine
that was in them, not because of the merely human.
To live at the spiritual level is to wage the terrible battle
of life without arms of one's own; to do all things in
the power of Him Who gives strength, having no power
of one's own. This is true courage. It is easy to fight
while there is something left that is one's very own. There
at least is something that can be wielded at will, something that can be turned against any foe no matter whence
he come. The child of God fights naked. He has looked
into his soul and found that alone it was nothing; he
has glimpsed the crown to be won and it was the All.

And turning Godwards he has cried "I will accept my nothingness. Do with me as Thou wilt. Destroy all in me that is not Thee. Cut deep into my soul; I am strong enough to bear it for love of Thee."

Man of himself has not the strength to enter this battle. Of himself he can fight while there remains a weapon that is his own. But when all that is his is lost, if he be to continue the struggle he must do so in the strength of another. If the battle be for the possession of God the strength he needs must be the strength of God. God must be the other who will lend to man the strength of his arm when his own has fallen powerless by his side. Man must learn to fight relying no longer on the power he thought was his, but on the Omnipotence which he knows is his Maker's. And so, he needs the gift of Fortitude. It must be the Holy Spirit Himself Who will strengthen and encourage man. For man is asked to fight, now not just as a man but as a God, as the adopted child of God. He is a member of God's family and has a right to all the resources of God in the battle he must wage. He fights not as a mere man but as the child of his Father Who will allow him to suffer no harm. He does not fight alone. God is with him, the Holy Spirit, the Spirit of Fortitude, is with him. He faces the world in the power of God. He bears the destruction of self in the power of God. He aspires to the possession of an eternal prize, again in the power of God. All that he does he does in the power of God, and hence he does it bravely, courageously, and with confidence of victory. He is the child of God and he knows that the very hairs of his head are numbered.

We find an example of the fortitude of this world, opposed to the Fortitude which is a gift, in the conduct of St Peter during the Passion of his Master. At the last

Supper he had made the proud boast: "I will lay down my life for Thee" (John xiv. 37). And if we consider the matter fairly, the boast can hardly be said to be a fantastic one. For St Peter loved his Master. And he was one of those simple country folk to whom loyalty is so common as almost to cease to be a virtue. At the moment of uttering those words he sincerely meant what he said; and it was not merely then that he meant them, for when Our Lord was taken prisoner in the garden of Olives St Peter sprang to his defence: "Then Simon Peter having a sword, drew it, and struck the servant of the High Priest, and cut off his right ear" (John xviii. 10).

We should note the precise significance of St Peter's action. It was but the logical consequence of the sincerity of his promise. He had promised to die for his Master, meaning thereby to do all in his power for his Master, even if death were the consequence. And so, when the danger really presents itself, he does the first thing that he, Peter, was capable of doing; he draws his sword, and facing the danger in the strength of Peter, attacks the envoys of the priests. Our Lord's remark to Peter is the first intimation that there is something too human in his way of acting: "Put up thy sword into the scabbard" (John xviii. 11). He does not deny the need for courage in the emergency, but He hints that there is courage of a kind which Peter does not understand too clearly. And Peter finds in his Master's words his first disillusionment.

If we turn to the twenty-sixth chapter of the Gospel according to St Matthew we see how Peter came to know fully the emptiness of the strength upon which he relied. He was brave enough to follow Our Lord even though he did remain afar off. But he followed as Peter, as the faithful friend, as one whose loyalty was

equal to any test. And then he denied his Master.
Peter's reawakening after the denial is narrated in
significant terms: "And going forth he wept bitterly"
(Matt. xxvi. 75). Why should he weep, were it not
that he had realized for the first time that of himself he
was nothing—that of himself he was unequal to the task
God had given him to perform. His tears were tears of
sorrow, it is true, tears of shame and regret—but they
were also the tears of a man who has learned that he is
only a child. Peter could weep now, he could come
to the empty tomb—but to do all this was the work of
love; strength had fled, and the spirit had not as yet
been given. For the moment he remains a spiritual
coward. He is sustained by hope and love, but he
lacks the power to advance. He has learned that of
himself he is but a reed swaying in the river of life—so
easy to crush or bruise, so helpless to repair its fall. And
then came Pentecost when Peter was filled with the
power of God: "And suddenly there came a sound from
heaven as of a mighty wind coming . . . and they were
all filled with the Holy Ghost" (Acts ii. 2–4). Once
more Peter was asked to confess that he knew the Lord
—this time the Lord crucified, abandoned, and despised.
"But Peter standing up with the eleven, lifted up his
voice and spoke to them . . . let all the house of Israel
know most certainly that God hath made both Lord
and Christ, this same Jesus, whom you have crucified"
(Acts ii. 14 and 36). This was the fulfilment of the
promise made to the Apostles by Our Lord: "But when
they shall deliver you up, take no thought how or what
to speak: for it shall be given you in that hour what to
speak. For it is not you that speak, but the Spirit of your
Father that speaketh in you" (Matt. x. 19–20). It was
no longer Peter that spoke, but the Holy Ghost that

spoke in him; it was no longer the strength of Peter that faced the onslaught of the power of darkness, but the strength of Him Who came as a mighty wind. Peter knew that his true strength was the strength of God, and that with God all things were possible.

This example taken from the life of St Peter reminds us that the field of action of Fortitude is not merely the inner struggle with self. This struggle may be the most violent and may persist when every other foe has fallen; but there are none the less other foes. There is the world and the devil. One man against the evil of the world, one man against the prince of the powers of darkness—such a man is doomed. Brave though he be, the odds are too unequal. He may be attacked on any side—in his good name, in his possessions, in his friends and family, in health of mind and body. And to all this he can oppose but the physical endurance of the highest of the animals and a spiritual firmness less than that of the lowest of the angels. If he face these foes in the might of his own arm and the strength of his own will he must surely fall. But he can face them in the strength and might of God his Father. He does not fight alone. There is One Who fights in and with him. "I can do all things in Him who strengtheneth me" (Phil. iv. 13).

True courage is a mean between opposed vices: foolhardiness and pusillanimity. The courageous man is not he who undertakes the impossible, nor is it he who shrinks from hurt; but it is he who, steering a middle course between rashness and fear, pursues the good in the measure of his strength. Since then courage may exist in either of two ways, it follows that true courage consists in the regulation of two impulses—fear's tendency to flight and folly's tendency to attack; and courage is shown in facing up to what may be overcome, and in bearing manfully what cannot be escaped. Now it is the peculiarity of all fortitude, whether virtue or gift, that its most perfect act is that of supporting the evil it cannot banish. At first sight it might appear that the man who attacks is braver than he who can merely hold his first position. But a little reflection upon one's own experience shows that this is not so. The heat and interest of the battle make wounds less hard to bear. What the soldier fears above all else is the state of siege, the long-drawn waiting and the sense of nameless fears. One feels a man while one is active. One knows that the danger is being faced and that it is after all but a human danger to be met by human weapons. But the danger that simply menaces, that is felt to crush and cannot be thrown off—this is the danger that calls for real heroism and this is the danger that lurks in spiritual experience.

For explain it away as we may wish, the spiritual life is one where we are more acted upon than acting. Self must die that God may be all in all. God has His infinite designs—designs of love and mercy—for each and every one of us and we must allow Him to work in us as He wills. But there is one thing that He wills for all called to holiness—the complete and unreserved resignation of self into His hands. This is the great heroic offering He asks of us; to commit ourselves without fear to His guidance. He may elect to lead us by unlit ways and alleys, He may guide us along a road where the deceiving glare of reason seems to reveal a thousand yawning pitfalls. We must let Him lead—and that is courage. To guide ourselves is to shrink from the sacrifice of trust.

It would, however, be an error to mistake this courageous bearing of trials for mere inactivity. It is, on the contrary, an intense form of living. Our Lord's attitude in the face of trials, His submission to the guidance of the Father, was not mere passive resignation. It was fortitude inspired by love. It was not because He could not resist His persecutors that He bore their harshness. "Thinkest thou," He said to St Peter, "that I cannot ask my Father, and He will give me presently more than twelve legions of angels." Our Lord had, what we have not, the power to overcome all difficulties. But He elected to bear them, as we must. He did all that the world might know that He loved the Father. He elected rather to be led than to lead Himself. But it was He Himself Who had made the choice and so His courage was not the resignation of despair but abandonment to love.

This is what God asks of us on earth and this it is that the Holy Ghost gives us in the gift of Fortitude. We must be strong through love and in love show our strength. We must love God and leave the struggle to His omnipotence. Nature will fret under this restraint and seeming inactivity. The urge to self-preservation will chafe under an attitude so opposed to what it would inspire. But we must love God sufficiently to know that all will be well. The child who fears the night knows no anxiety if it but hold its father's hand, for then it has his strength to ward off evil. God asks the same thing of us. The child loves its father, and safe in the utter trustworthiness of him it loves, ventures where dread dwelt before. Love must give us courage to face death and danger. And Love is the Spirit of Him "that raised up Jesus from the dead".

CHAPTER VI

THE GIFT OF COUNSEL

*" Be ye therefore wise as serpents and simple as
doves."* (Matt x. 16.)

It may have seemed strange to some to find a chapter
on a gift such as Fortitude placed between those devoted
to Wisdom and Counsel. For both Wisdom and Counsel
are perfections of the intellect, whereas Fortitude perfects
the appetitive part of man. Would it not then appear
more logical to treat of Counsel before Fortitude and so
preserve a certain unity of subject-matter?

Whatever be the force of this objection—and it may
be admitted frankly that it would be far from negligible
if this purported to be a purely scientific study of the
gifts, and not an ascetical one as well—this order has
been selected with a definite purpose in view: to bring
home to the reader the distance that there may be
between the speculative acceptance of truth and its
practical application. We have just seen that to live the
principles dictated by Wisdom demands courage of a
divine order, and that without this courage the assent
of the mind to principles will remain a matter of mind
alone, which, never reaching as far as the will, leaves
the whole man, the man whom God made as striving
after perfection through the willed acceptance of the life
of grace, crippled and misshapen. This revelation of
the insufficiency of cold reason prepares the way for
another truth: the gifts of Understanding, Wisdom, and
Knowledge are not sufficient even on the side of the intellect

for the untrammelled activity of the child of God. There is required as well, in the intellect itself, the added gift of Counsel.

That there is this need is evident on the analogy of what we may have noticed ourselves time after time in men with whom we have come in contact. It is not an unusual experience to meet men who seem to have intellectual attainments well above the average but who achieve nothing of note in practical life. They have mastered the details of some profession or other in such a way as to be able to expose all the principles underlying it with perfect accuracy. They may, in addition, be men of natural courage. They do not fear to take a risk, and when things seem to turn against them, they have powers of endurance capable of enabling them to weather the storm. And yet, it not infrequently happens that such men do not succeed. They may be capable teachers, but never seem to be quite what is wanted when a first-class appointment is to be made. They may be excellent lawyers—going from success to success in the academic field of preliminary examinations. They may be brilliant doctors, whose degrees are the envy of their less gifted fellows. But something seems to be lacking. They do not seem to have the power to apply their knowledge to the concrete case that presents itself. They are masters in the art of unwinding the threads of knotted speculation, but the simple coils into which the coarse rope of everyday existence falls so naturally are far too unwieldy for their sensitive fingers. Such a teacher will ever remain in a second-rate school, in spite of the fact that there will be no doubt about his superior instruction; such a lawyer will, if no worse fate befall him, die, poor but honest, in a small town; such a doctor will attain a reputation for eccentricity and erudition, but will never make his fortune. They lack, in each case, the power of dealing with the concrete event.

For it must be understood that the determination of the course of action to be adopted in presence of concrete circumstances is something more than the mere grasping of the principles which guide it. It is not sufficient for a doctor to know that if one kind of symptoms is present the disease is pneumonia, whereas if they be of another kind, the disease is pleurisy. He must be able to state with certainty that the symptoms which he finds in the sick man present are those of one or the other sickness. It is poor consolation to the sick man to know that the doctor he has called in is capable of prescribing the best treatment for any conceivable illness if only he can decide which one it is that demands treatment here and now. To deal with the concrete case one needs to be able to weigh the conflicting claims of different items of evidence. One characteristic of the event may suggest that it falls under one heading; another may incline one to believe that it is of a totally different kind. To decide which outweighs the other is not a matter of grasping abstract principles. It is a matter of deciding which of two or more principles is applicable at all. And then it may easily happen that not two but many principles may appear to be involved. And then the question is more difficult still.

One may note this difficulty often in cases of relations between man and man. You may be called upon to do business with a person who is a complete stranger. Suppose that there is a great deal at stake and that it is absolutely essential to your success to obtain the support of the man you are interviewing. He does not seem to fall in readily with your views—in fact, he seems, if anything, to be determined to oppose you with all his power. Now it can easily happen that he will impress you as being of either of two temperaments: he will be either blusterer or man of determination. The success of your enterprise depends on your finding out which of these temperaments is really his, and acting accordingly. His air of confidence seems exaggerated; so he must be a blusterer. But then, strength gives confidence, and there appears to be behind all his bravado that element of calm which is the index to strength. What attitude must be adopted in his regard? Bluff can be beaten down, but opposition only eggs on strength. Strength will listen to reason but bluff will mistake reason for weakness. And how can one decide which of all the contradictory notes gives the key to the character they veil. The decision rests with a special faculty—an intellectual faculty that is pre-eminently practical—the intellectual endowment known as prudence.

Prudence is necessary to tread the maze of practical life with assurance. It is the link between the abstract and the fact; between thought and life. Those who lack it are like ships that toss propellerless on angry seas: the perfection of their equipment will never save them if there be no possibility of bringing that equipment to bear upon the heaving waves. And yet, there is a kind of escape for imprudent souls—if they have but prudence enough to avail themselves of it. It is that they seek counsel when they are in doubt. If their own prudence be not sufficient to guide them, let them commit themselves to the prudence of a better and a wiser man. Their journey will be inglorious, but safe. They will stray from the road when they cannot find their guide; but with him once more at their side they will return to the sure path. They will have lost the thrill of venturing unaided, but they will have found the quiet peace of confiding love.

Now there can be no doubt that the spiritual life is a field where prudence will find ample matter for her intervention. The moment a person begins to study spiritual books he is struck by the multitude of rules of conduct which they lay down and the frequent irreconcilability of a number of these rules. One book may recommend keeping a kind of diary in which to note spiritual progress and failure. Another condemns this as leading to introspection and lack of confidence in divine providence. Another would approve of the idea, but would recommend two books: one, a plain book, for ordinary, commonplace facts, and the other, more ornate, for the great graces received. And then, is it not said that the greatest help to love of God is the constant recollection of the graces He has given us, whereas it is also true that nothing could be better for the soul than the remembrance of her past sins and infidelity. In the presence of all this conflicting theory, what is the soul to do? Keep a diary or not keep a diary; note in it her sins or her graces?

It might perhaps be objected that the difficulty exposed just now is not inherent in the spiritual life but is due rather to the defective manner in which it is exposed by spiritual writers, who neglect to point out that the practices they advise are good only for certain types of persons. The introspective type will make more progress without a diary; the hard-headed man of business will profit by a little spiritual accountancy. The spiritual life will then be a simple matter for whoever has decided upon his temperament and the general lines of action in keeping with it.

The objection is as unsound as it is plausible. There are few things more difficult for an individual to decide than what exactly his temperament is. Most temperaments are mixed. They contain a dash of melancholy, of courage, of timidity, of sheer sloth, and it is always to a great extent a problem which element is in control at a given moment. And then there are certain situations which must be faced no matter what be one's temperament. It is better for the hotheaded man to keep in the background. But there are moments when he must come to the fore, and on such occasions he is forced to play with fire and yet not be burned. The slothful should beware of sluggish inaction. But at times one must play a waiting game and still not sink into pure inactivity. Were it well for the slothful always to act and for the headstrong to stand back the issue would be clear cut. But life is not a copy-book exercise, and often the man whose salvation seems to lie in peace is forced to the forefront of a social struggle.

The spiritual life which all must live calls then for prudence, and failing this for counsel. The spiritual life calls for a gift—and being a gift it can be no other than Counsel. The child of God is called to live a new life in new surroundings. He is called to regulate that life in accordance with principles that he has learned. He is assailed on all sides by enemies. He finds that there are in himself tendencites to sin and turn away from God, of which he had no idea before. Faced with new problems, torn by new interior struggles, the child of God must seek advice at every step; and to Whom shall he turn if not to the Spirit That guides him, to the Holy Ghost, the Spirit of counsel. The Holy Ghost is ever at his side telling him what to do, showing what is to be avoided in the evil that threatens, showing what is good in the situation that seems so strange, telling how the Father may be loved and served there where He seems to have no place, giving confidence and assurance in the solving of life's practical riddles.

For confidence, intellectual sureness in the face of situations that call for decisive action—these are the fruits of the gift of Counsel. Our Lord had foretold this when He uttered those words to His disciples: "And when they shall lead you and deliver you up, be not thoughtful beforehand what you shall speak; but whatsoever shall be given you in that hour, that speak ye. For it is not you that speak but the Holy Ghost" (Mark xiii. 11). There will be no hesitation. What ought I to say? Ought I to speak at all? The Holy Ghost is there with His gift of Counsel. He knows the mind of God. He sees the right side of that pattern of life which to us is a maze of knots, and knows the divine design that gives meaning to every broken line and change of colour. The Holy Ghost is God, and so He understands fully the situation in which we find ourselves. He can give us the counsel we need. He can show us how to make all things work unto good. Under His guidance we see the course that God has mapped out for us at every moment of the day. There is no fevered questioning, no doubt, no half-advance half-retreat. God's will is clear to us and God's grace will make that divine will possible of accomplishment. The Holy Ghost makes life an ordered whole, from the deepest of its mysteries to the most trivial of its events.

Holy Scripture—if we read it in the light of the Holy Spirit—is full of the complexity of life and man's insufficiency to smooth out its tangles unaided. St James tells us of the difficulty of regulating the tongue: "And the tongue is a fire, a world of iniquity. The tongue is placed among our members, which defileth the whole body, and inflameth the wheel of our nativity, being set on fire by hell. For every nature of beasts, and of birds, and of serpents, and of the rest, is tamed, and hath been tamed by the nature of man: But the tongue no man can tame, an unquiet evil, full of deadly poison" (James iii. 6-9). Who has not learned the truth of these words in living his own life? How often have we not spoken when silence had been better? How often have we not begun to speak, and finding that our words were ill-chosen have blundered on, hoping for the best, when an apology would have been more appropriate? And then there have been words uttered in hasty anger. It was easy to persuade oneself in the heat of passion that then or never was the moment to take a firm stand; that too many wrongs had been suffered and that it was really in the best interests of all concerned to put the wrongdoer once and for ever into the place to which he belonged. Admirable maxims, utterly true as speculative principles—but is this the moment for applying them? And is it in the smoke of battle that we may best descry the true lineaments of the features of a foe? The tongue must be guided by Counsel if it be to speak only to the glory of God the Father and in love of the neighbour. Of itself it wavers between curse and blessing: "By it we bless God and the Father: and by it we curse men who are made after the likeness of God" (James iii. 9).

St Paul speaks of the dangers that lurk in the observance of positive law: "Now him that is weak in faith, take unto you: not in disputes about thoughts. For one believeth that he may eat all things: but he that is weak let him eat herbs. Let not him that eateth despise him that eateth not, and he that eateth not, let him not judge him that eateth. For God hath taken him to Him" (Rom. xiv. 1-3). One of the pitfalls into which the fervent beginner is liable to fall—just as it is the last of the preoccupations of the tepid—is a slavish literalness in the observance of what is of positive precept or of mere counsel. By positive precept I mean now, only that which is of human origin. Divine positive law does not come up for discussion here. And slavish literalness in the application of such precepts and commands can be harmful both to others and to oneself.

It is harmful to others when it leads us to impose upon them an obligation which has no objective justification, or when it leads us to question their free use of the liberty God has really given them. Souls have been tortured because of well-meaning pious folk who insisted that true spirituality consisted in certain practices to which they felt no attraction. The practices may be good. They may be recommended by the highest authorities. But why impose them where they are likely to do harm and in the name of a binding force which they have not got? The pious man who in season and out of season preaches the devotions that happen to appeal to himself at his neighbours, needs the gift of Counsel. There will be occasions when his advice will be accepted. But there will be others when it will be out of place, and he must learn to discern the one from the other. Better still, let him allow the Holy Ghost to do the discerning; for the Holy Ghost has the sanctification of his neighbour at heart, even more than he has; and He will take care to inspire at the right moment the words that will touch and inflame.

There is need of Counsel also when we feel called upon to disturb the good faith of those who do wrong while thinking that their actions contain no evil. There will be times when the duty to point out the right to them will be clear; and this happens most easily when one is bound in virtue of one's office to do so. But there will be occasions when doubts will arise. Will my advice be accepted? Will more harm than good be the result of my intervention? Will he continue to act as he has ever acted in spite of the fact that he now knows that he should no longer do so? And then, unless we have the gift of Counsel, we falter, omitting good, or causing evil.

A striking case of the working of the gift of Counsel is revealed in 1 Cor. ii. 1–2: "And, I, brethren, when I came to you, came not in loftiness of speech or of wisdom, declaring unto you the testimony of Christ. For I judged myself not to know anything among you, but Jesus Christ, and Him crucified." St Paul was at grips with the world-old problem: "Is my work to be entirely the work of God or must man play a part?" And this is a problem which on every occasion demands a new answer. For though our work is to be the work of God, the human element must vary according as God sees well to use it or to lay it aside. St Paul could have endeavoured to impress the Corinthians with his learning—and we know that when God so inspired him, he did not hesitate to draw attention to the fact that he had studied under the great teacher Gamaliel. But God wished that his preaching to the Corinthians be in the power of Christ crucified and not in the power of the wisdom of Paul. And so he came not in loftiness of speech. He did nothing to show that he should be heard, that his words, even humanly speaking, carried authority. He just preached Christ crucified and allowed the beauty of the Crucified to soften hearts that authority would but have flattered.

It would be a pleasant task to show the workings of Counsel in the Apostle of the gentiles: how he who went so fearlessly to death did not disdain to escape in a

basket when as yet there was work to do (2 Cor. xi. 33);
how he who looked upon himself as the last of all did
not hesitate to rebuke the great St Peter to his face
when he seemed to yield to the ultra-jewish party in
the early church (Gal. ii. 14). But let us turn instead
to Him Who was ever full of the Holy Ghost and see in
the person of Our Lord the model of the child of God,
led by the Spirit of Counsel.

Our Lord Himself told us that He was meek and
humble of heart; He would not crush the bruised reed.
And yet we find that He acted with courage and decision
when the Spirit revealed to Him that so He might the
better obtain the glory of God. "And when He was
entered into the temple, he began to cast out them that
sold and bought in the temple, and overthrew the tables
of the money changers, and the chairs of them that sold
doves. And he suffered not that any man should carry
a vessel through the temple" (Mark xi. 15–16). How
we should have hesitated and deliberated before taking
such a drastic step. Perhaps it would be well to remon-
strate with the sellers? Perhaps to interfere with them
in any way at all would only provoke indecorous scenes
in the House of God? With Our Lord there is no
faltering, no doubt. He is full of the Spirit of God, the
Spirit of Counsel, and guided by the Spirit judges
promptly and confidently that now is the moment for
action and that the time for soft words is no more.

Have you ever considered Our Lord's attitude to the
different questions put Him at the time of His most
Holy Passion, as a lesson in counsel? How He answered
some and left others unheard? There was in His attitude
no suspicion of a rigid application of a rule. He did not
reply because one should never remain silent, nor was
He silent because silence is always better than words.

He spoke and was silent as the Spirit gave Him to do, with a marvellous suppleness and adaptability which we can only suspect but which prayerful meditation may, partly at least, reveal. It is in prayer rather than in study that we shall come to know the gift of Counsel; for Counsel is a gift of God and only the prayer of God lays bare its secrets.

And then there was His sublime mercy to the sinful woman who dared to anoint His feet and wipe them with her hair (John xii. 3). Judas was indignant—and who of us can say that he would not have been at least surprised? Yet Our Lord's defence of her action was unfaltering. He was sure of Himself, when mere man could not be sure. And His sureness was the sureness of the gift of Counsel.

We have seen how St Paul dared to dispense with all human aids in preaching the gospel. It is the same St Paul who indicates that in this he is only following his Master: "For you know the grace of Our Lord Jesus Christ, that being rich He became poor and despised: . . . emptied himself taking the form of a servant . . ." (Phil. ii. 7). He was the Power of God but He came in the weakness of poor human flesh. We may imagine that had He lived among men in the majesty of His Thabor glory, they would have heard Him; they would perhaps have heard Him had He even revealed His Divinity to men from time to time with such evidence as to compel submission. But He chose another way, a way that only God could see was the best, a way that appeared folly in the eyes of men and paved the way for the death upon the Cross. But how could men have known that the Cross was a throne and that He that hung thereon was even then coming into His kingdom?

We are the adopted children of God. But we lack the *savoir faire* of the child born into its family. We simply do not see what is expected of a child of God in the complex circumstances of real life. As was the case with every other of our needs, this need has been supplied by the Holy Spirit. He lends us His divine *savoir faire;* He gives us, and leads us by, the gift of Counsel. "With expectation I have waited for the Lord, and he was attentive to me. And he heard my prayers and brought me out of the pit of misery and the mire of dregs. And he set my feet upon a rock and directed my steps" (Ps. xxxix. 2–3).

CHAPTER VII

THE GIFT OF PIETY

"Abba, Father." (Rom. viii. 15.)

There are few more touching lines in the Church's liturgy, than those sung at the close of Compline, the official night-prayer of the child of God: I mean the "In manus tuas, Domine, commendo spiritum meum"—"Into Thy hands, Lord, I commend my spirit." Even if we abstract from the singular beauty of the melody to which the words are sung, even if we refuse to embody them in any image smacking of sentiment, or of mere "human-ness", they are rich in suggestion of a relationship between God and man that reason could never have suspected.

For reason's attitude to God is to see in Him the First Cause, the Being from Whom we come, on Whom we depend, and to Whose glory we are ordained whether we will it or not. Reason arrives at the knowledge of God through the consideration that things must have had a cause that explains them fully; and that cause is known by the name of God. But man himself is one of the caused beings—man is one of the phenomena whose very make-up declares that they are dependent on something higher. And so man comes to know God as the Being on Whom he depends—the Being Who gave him all that he has. The universe is the creature of God. He drew it from nothing. He gained nothing by having made it; He will remain the same when all things will have passed. The beauty of the world has no power to move Him—for in relation to Him it is but nothingness.

Man cannot influence Him, for man has nothing but what He gives. God, we are only too prone to think, must be indifferent to man's weal or woe, for He stands far apart from the pain and strain of human effort.

Revelation has painted for us a far different picture of the Almighty. We hear of a First Cause Who suffers death for His creatures; of an Immortal God Who died upon a cross. We hear of a far-off Deity Who came on earth and lived for three and thirty years in the midst of the sons of men; Who did not disdain to have as Mother one drawn from the race that had offended Him and that would condemn Him to death. All this and more is contained in those lines of Compline. God is no longer far from us. He is near, even at the door of our souls. To Him we confide ourselves when at the close of day we feel strength decline and our weakness calls for a support. We know that God is the support we need. Though God, He loves us. We are His children. In His hands we are safe—safer far than if we were committed to our own unaided care. God has come down to our level. He is no longer the Cause Whose brightness sends no ray darting through the realms of created space: He has become the loving shepherd of weak human souls.

Attractive though this idea of God be, its full practical acceptance is a difficult matter. There seems at first sight in some mysterious way, to be a greater sense of security in looking on God as a Master than in regarding Him as a Friend. And yet the mystery of this is not so very hard to understand. It finds its explanation in the fact, to which we have so often referred, that our sonship through grace is merely adoptive.

Suppose that a child be adopted into the family of a person who, for a certain number of years, was its father's employer, or landlord. The child has grown up into a certain attitude of servility. It has been taught to respect the authority of him on whom the daily bread or the family roof depended. When the master appeared he was to be treated with a certain deferential self-abasement. After all, everything depended on him, and the realities of life demanded that this be recognized. Then comes the time when the child is accepted into the master's family as if it were one of his own flesh and blood. The relationship has been changed, but the old attitude will remain. In place of the affectionate respect due to him as a father, the benefactor will continue to receive the servile obedience of a dependant. There will be nothing of that spontaneous reverential trust that characterizes the child born into the family. Services will be rendered—but they will be the services of a subject; rules will be respected—but rather in fear than in love; little gifts may be made—but they will take the form of peace-offerings, or even bribes! Respect will be rather supine cringing; fear will take the place of love.

Since God has granted us a revelation of Himself and we have accepted this revelation through the gift of faith, certain of the extreme errors in the attitude to God outlined in the opening paragraph of this chapter are excluded in our case. We know that God is not without interest in man; that though He finds in Himself all that He needs for His own full and perfect happiness, He has not disdained to give a share in that happiness to creatures outside Himself. But one danger looms large on the horizon of the man who approaches God with faith and hope and refuses to give full sway to the greatest of all virtues, charity: He will see in God, the Creator and the Master, and will forget, in the practical ruling of his life, that even though God be Creator and Master

He is before all else a Father to the soul He has adopted by grace. The error consists thus in giving to the virtue of religion the place which belongs by right to love, the queen of all the virtues. It means that the soul has stopped at what should be the entry to the spiritual life, and refuses to go beyond, into the joy that is hers now but for the taking. In other words, the soul experiences the same difficulty in seeing God as a Father, that we have remarked in the child adopted into the family of one on whom it depended before.

It is a fact that the entry to the spiritual life—for many souls at least, if not for most—is the conviction of dependence on God. For years we have felt our own masters. There were, of course, human beings who had a certain power of controlling our lives. But there were realms over which they had no rights; there were moments of the day which were altogether ours, to do and act as we wished. These were the moments when we were really our own masters. It was of these moments we thought when the stress of life began to tell—when others became importunate. Though we were at their beck and call for hours each day, there came at length a time when we had no master but our own wills. And the sweetness of this time dulled, or even made imperceptible, the bitterness of other hours; it was our moment of escape, of glorious, untrammelled freedom.

For years, too, we may have looked on God as just one of those masters who have a right to a certain section of our time and of our lives. The moments of prayer are to be given to Him, the moment of assistance at Holy Mass. Throughout the whole day He must be considered, it is true, to the extent that He may not be offended. But provided we did not offend Him we saw no reason why we should not take a holiday from the service of God from time to time, just as we took a holiday from the service of any other master. And so we came to look on holiday-time, hours of recreation, parties, dinners, and suchlike matters as things in which God had no say. He must not be offended during them, but there was no reason why we should not use them as occasions of escaping His vigilance and living within the pale of what He permitted, as if in such matters the ultimate bar of judgment was our own selves.

The soul's first awakening to the fallacy of this reasoning comes not infrequently when it realizes in some blinding flash of God-given light that there is no instant of its life when it does not depend on God and when it has not positive obligations to live just as He wishes. It may be that the soul will be seized by the idea of God's presence in the world and His awareness of all our doings; it may be that the soul will be faced by the fact that at every moment of its existence it depends on God, that every thought and action depends on Him; or it may be that God will reveal Himself to it as a Judge Who will weigh every idle word and deed, Whose vigilance nothing can escape. Whatever be the precise form the revelation of God may take, one thing will be clear: the soul is no longer its own master; at every instant of every day it stands in the presence of a Lord and God Whose rights are absolute and far-reaching. The soul will struggle before it will admit this truth: there is nothing we treasure more than the power of self-determination. But if it be generous, the result will be a donation of self to God without conscious reserve—a complete immolation of life to the service of the Divine Majesty to the extent to which God will show that there are sacrifices to be made. As far as the soul is concerned, there will be no holding back. It will give all it sees should be given. But there will remain secret treasures of self-love that only grace and time will reveal and which God will not ask it to give up as yet lest He crush the bruised reed that is human generosity.

The soul in the ecstasy of its first total offering of self to God, its Lord and Master, feels nothing of the servility of its relationship with Him, nor of the grudging nature of the offering it makes. It does not see that it has done nothing more than to accept its creaturehood—a great and generous act, it is true, but still far short of what God wants. Nor does it see that its offering is not so acceptable in God's eyes as He wishes it to be; He asks the devotion of a child and receives the extorted service of a bondman. In fact, generous though this act may be, considered relatively to the weakness of him who makes it, it falls far short of what God wishes. He wishes to be served as a Lord Who is a Father. Our devotion to Him should be, not forced by weight of argument, but gushing forth and overflowing from the fount of love. Such devotion is more radical than that of a bondman however faithful. For love knows no limits. And when love is the mainspring of reverence, reverence issues in complete surrender, in devoted service. Love is keenly awake to the rights of a superior. Where the paid servant sees only what is expected of him, the loving son sees what his father deserves. Both serve to the extent to which they perceive their obligations. But one, viewing life from the angle of obligation sees necessarily far less than the other who views it as a means to add fuel to the fire of love that burns within his soul.

To consider God, then, as Lord and Master, necessary though it may be in the early stages of the spiritual life, when God must seize us by force, as it were, and tear us from this world, is of its very nature destined to lead to

regarding Him as a Father. It is not the final stage. The
precise meaning of this should be carefully noted. It
is not equivalent to saying that reverence must lead to
love. This is of course true; but it is not our present
problem. When we say that religion (the virtue which
leads us to accept practically God's dominion over us)
leads to Piety (the gift of the Holy Ghost) what we mean
is that one kind of service, respect, cult, must be gradually
replaced by another. God Who was at the beginning
honoured as Lord and Master must now be honoured
as Father; the rights we are now bound to respect are
those which every child sees in its parents—though, of
course, they exist in God far more perfectly than they
do in any earthly parent; the motive for our self-oblation
to God, our entire devotion of life to His service, must be
the fact that He is Our Father Who is in Heaven and
that all we have and are is the fruit of His loving care.
Progress in the spiritual life, therefore, does not mean
that we cease after a while to revere God; that the final
stage is one of easy intimacy. It means that our reverence
must grow from that of a creature into that of a child.
It remains reverence; but becomes reverence of a new
and higher kind. It is true that God still remains our
Creator, and that we owe Him adoration and service
under that title; but He is before all else the Father of
those in the state of grace, and they must learn to integrate
all other titles of reverence into that of Father. God
is not just a Creator, and a Father as well. He is a Father
Who has created us, a Creator Who has adopted us,
and we must love and serve as Father, Him Who has
first revealed Himself as Creator. For the gifts of the Holy
Ghost are higher than the moral Virtues—even the
infused ones. And so our religion[1] must become the

---

[1] i.e. the virtue of religion.

tool of our Piety.[1] We must give God the cult and service due to a Master and Lord, in the spirit of childhood. We can never forget our dependence upon Him as the Being Who drew us out of nothingness. But we accept it in a burst of childlike devotion. What is of prime importance for us is that God is Our Father. He may be Our Maker as well—but it is ultimately His Fatherhood that counts in our eyes, for we see even in the fact that He drew us out of nothing a revelation more of a Father's love than of a God's Omnipotence.

Piety then, in the sense of a gift of the Holy Ghost, is a power given us of submitting ourselves to the Holy Ghost breathing into our souls a spirit of childlike reverence for Our Heavenly Father and of devotion to the furthering of His interests. It is not precisely what is meant in current usage by piety. The word is commonly taken to express in a general way a psychological attitude which embraces any and every virtue and practice of the spiritual life. As a gift it means the willed acceptance of God as our Father and of the obligations arising from His Fatherhood, under the guidance of the Holy Ghost. It has nothing in common with sentiment; nor even directly with fervour. But it sweetens life—for it is easy to serve a Father—and leads to generosity—since the good son is unreserved in his devotion to his father. Of itself, too, it does not mean loving God as Our Father; for to love God is the exclusive privilege of the virtue of charity. It is concerned entirely with the acceptance of God's right to service, of His Majesty; but it adds this of its own to what is done by the virtue of religion, that for it the rights and Majesty of God are the rights and Majesty of a Father, not just those of a Creator with Whom we have no community

[1] i.e. the gift of Piety.

of life and on Whom we should depend as being outside the family circle which is opened only by grace.

It is a striking fact that when Our Lord and Saviour taught His disciples and us how to pray, He taught us to address God as "Our Father Who art in heaven." The prayer He taught was an answer to the humble and trusting request: "Lord teach us how to pray." It was in the Saviour's mind a complete answer to that request. He meant it to be an adequate expression of what should be the attitude of the Christian in the presence of Almighty God. And it opens with the words "Our Father Who art in Heaven." There is no room for the objection that after all the Lord's prayer was meant just to be the expression of the Christian's love of God. It was meant to be that—but it was meant to be the expression of his attitude of dependence upon Him as well. For it includes explicit reference to dependence upon God: Hallowed be Thy name; give us this day our daily bread; lead us not into temptation. God's Name is worthy of praise because it is the name of the Infinite Majesty; we ask God for our daily bread because it is on Him that we depend at every moment of our existence for everything of which we stand in need; we ask Him not to lead us into temptation for we are in the hollow of His Hand, to be dealt with as He wills. Thus the fact that we depend on God and that we turn to Him in recognition of this dependence is at the very root of the prayer. But we are invited to turn to God not as Creator but as Father. He is both; we depend on Him under both titles. But of the two there is one which is particularly dear to Him—that of Father. For He is the Creator of the whole universe—of the earth and sea and stars. But to none of these things is He a Father as He is Father of the child adopted through grace. That favour

He has reserved for man alone among the beings of this earth; and it were churlishness in man to refuse to see in God what makes Him most worthy of service and praise.

The piety which Our Lord taught when He taught the disciples how to pray is a gift of the Holy Ghost: "For you have not received the spirit of bondage again in fear; but you have received the spirit of adoption of sons, whereby we cry: Abba (Father)" (Rom. viii. 15). Our Lord was Son by nature. He always acted as a son should act. When the Jews accused Him of being possessed by a devil, He said: "I have not a devil but I honour my Father . . ." (John viii. 49). His whole life was devoted to the service of His Father: "As the Father hath given me commandment so do I" (John xiv, 31). And the Father saw and took pleasure in His attitude of filial devotion: "Thou art my beloved Son: in Thee I am well pleased" (Mark i. 11). It is the Spirit of the Lord Who will inspire us with the same attitude of childlike reverence. The Spirit that led Our Saviour must lead us also, must raise us from that state of servile and self-seeking abjection to that of devoted sonship. We are no longer slaves but free "by the freedom wherewith Christ has made us free" (Gal. iv. 31). Our freedom is "libertas"—the quality of the "liberi" or children of God. It is a freedom won for us by Our Saviour and conferred on us by His Spirit. It is a freedom which binds us to God as we were never bound before, and could never be bound by any other tie—for it is the freedom of children, heirs to all the possessions of their Father, walking as masters in their Father's house, using His riches as if they were their own: but doing all this in love and reverence, in a spirit of dutiful devotion and affectionate generosity.

We have just referred to using the treasures of Our

Father's house in a spirit of filial piety, and there is implicit in this remark the truth that piety extends not merely to our relations with God, but everything else as well, in so far as it may be regarded as belonging in some way to the Father and hence worthy of being treated with respect. There is an exceedingly beautiful parable in the Gospel of St Luke which illustrates this point better than human words could ever do. It is the parable of the master of the vineyard (Luke xx. 9–16). The master had let his vineyard to certain husbandmen. And after a time he sent a servant to collect what was due to him. The husbandmen, however, attacked the servant and sent him away without payment. And they meted out similar treatment to two others who were sent on the same errand. Then the master—though he had certainly the right to deliver the husbandmen up to judgment—decided to attempt to win them by kindness: "What shall I do?" he enquired. "I will send my beloved son: It may be, when they see him, they will reverence him." He sent his son clothed in the dignity of the father, believing that they would respect him on that account.

God never ceases to act that way with us. Every soul in the state of grace is His beloved son, and hence entitled to reverent treatment at our hands. When we mix with our fellow men we do not mix with mere mortals; we move among the beloved children of Our Heavenly Father. On that account every slight offered to them, every unkind treatment, every wilful disregard of their rights and dignity, becomes an offence against the majesty of the Father Whose children they are. The man who hardens his heart and refuses to aid the poor, even if He cannot see in them the image of their Saviour, should be able to see in them the children of His God;

and if he treats them unworthily it is their Father and his Whom he has offended more than anyone else. Every person, everything in the world is consecrated by the fact that it belongs to God. Piety should then characterize our attitude to both men and things. The ground which we tread, no matter where it be, is an ambassador of Our Heavenly Father. Our piety can know no bounds. It extends as far as does the dominion of God—that is to say to every creature without exception that has come from His hands, to every soul without exception whose Father He is.

The gift of Piety finds, of course, obvious expression in our attitude to persons and things which stand in immediate relationship to the Divine Majesty. As examples we may refer to the persons of the Saints and the word of Scripture. The saints are particularly dear to Almighty God. It was He and none other who adorned them with the gifts of grace that we admire in them, and hence, in recognizing their dignity, we do nothing more than admire and praise the works of Our Father Himself. There is nothing in the saints worthy of our devotion which does not come from God. To praise the saints is to praise Him Who made them to be what they are; to disregard the saints is to withdraw one's attention from precisely that section of the universe in which God is most active, in which there is nothing but what He put there. It is, in other words, to be failing in piety; to be indifferent to the preferences of Our Father; to wish to subordinate His interests to ours rather than to take interest in what He says is of supreme interest for Himself. And what we have said of the saints is a thousand times more true if applied to Our Blessed Lady. God so loved her as to make her His Mother. There is nothing in her that does not come from Him;

in fact, He has worked in her soul with such loving care for detail, with such a conscious effort after perfection, that she is His masterpiece. How then can we dare to think that our filial attitude to Our Father lacks nothing if we have no love for her whom He loves beyond all the sons of men. Earthly children humour their parents by taking a polite interest in their fads and hobbies, even if these latter be trivial in themselves. God has shown that Mary was—always, of course, after His Divine Son —His great interest. If it is praiseworthy in children of an earthly father to waste their time in trivialities just through a sense of filial devotion, is it a defect in a child of God, to vow himself to her whom His Heavenly Father has made Mother of God, Mother of men, Queen of heaven, Dispensatrix of all graces? To be lacking in devotion to Mary is to fail in piety to God. To refuse to be devout to her as a child should be to its mother is again to be lacking in piety to Him, because He made her to be our mother. Piety is a gift which, concentrating the soul on God its Father, makes it big enough and warm enough to embrace all mankind and the angels and saints as well.

To explain how the gift of Piety should animate our attitude to the Person of Our Saviour would take more space and time than can be provided in the present work. It is a question for treatment at a later date. But a word may be said in passing on piety and the Holy Scriptures.

The books of the Old and New Testament contain the word of God Himself. Hence they should be respected with delicate consideration. We should not use quotations from Scripture as material for witticisms. That treatment is unworthy of their author. Nor should we do—as even pious people do at times—formulate arguments on religious subjects, and then, by way of afterthought adduce a text, usually to be understood in an accommodated sense, having no authority other than that it strikes us as ingenious. If we wish to argue from the authority of the inspired word let us use texts which were really meant by Almighty God to convey the idea we intend to convey, and then let us give them pride of place. There is a certain lack of delicacy in using the authority of Our Father in Heaven in a way which indicates a desire to shut the mouths of the opposition by moving a kind of closure which they will feel bound to accept, but which they know is only a buttress to the feebleness of our arguments. If the authority of God be called into the arena, this should be only when the words which have His authority are clearly to be understood in the sense we mean, and when they are adduced as being of divine weight. God's word should never be used to adorn our own views. To do so is to make little of Our Father.

Piety, in the sense in which we have described it in this chapter, is a gift of the Holy Ghost Who lives in us through charity. In fact it is because we love God and are His friends that our respect for Him must be that due to a Father. Piety, in other words, is a special manifestation of love. Were God not our friend, had He not allowed us to share in His Divine nature we could never look on Him as a Father, but only as Lord and Master. Once, however, He had made Himself our Friend He has become Father as well, and the test of our love and friendship is the thoroughness with which we accept our dependence upon Him, Our Father. We must love God—and while we remain on earth there is no more perfect act than that of love. But love must be completed—though not perfected—by the homage and respect due to Him as Father. This is what St Thomas means when, in a striking passage he speaks of piety as a "protestatio caritatis"—a protestation of love. It is love that makes a Father out of a Creator; if we wilfully persist in regarding God principally as Creator we are shutting our hearts to the greatest mystery of His love for us. God wishes us to be His children. Why should we strive to remain forever under the spell of a principle which applies as truly to the grass of the fields as to the soul in the state of grace—the fact of creature-hood? Let us follow the invitation of Our Father. To do so is not to make the task of life objectively easier. More sacrifices are demanded of a son than of a hireling. But it is to lessen the strain and the toil. We shall give more, but count it less—for we shall give in love and childlike devotion and giving shall not count the cost.

CHAPTER VIII

THE GIFT OF FEAR

"And He shall be filled with the spirit of the fear of the Lord."
(Isaias, xi. 3.)

To mistake Piety for the Fear of the Lord and the Fear of the Lord for Piety is both common and understandable. For both take their origin from the fact of God's elevation above man. But whereas Piety sees this elevation as the dignity of a Father to Whose service life should be devoted—and hence finds its expression in cult and self-oblation—Fear of the Lord regards the Divine Majesty as capable of inflicting harm on us in some way —whether it be by punishment in the next world or by the pain of loss—and so finds expression in reverence towards God and distrust in that self, which, and which alone, can lead to the evils that come from the Hand of The Almighty. Piety does not fear God: it serves Him. Fear does not lead immediately to service; its real fruit is to empty us of self.

These prefatory remarks are necessary for the proper understanding of what is about to follow. It will happen here, as it has happened in the preceding chapter, that terms more strictly applicable to piety will be used of fear and vice versa. That this should be is inevitable. For there is no vocabulary which is valid for the one to the strict exclusion of the other. And yet there is little danger of error if the main principles be grasped. All that is required is a certain common sense in the understanding of isolated remarks. They must be read in a context of piety or fear as the case may be. And the same formula will have different meanings in different contexts. This warning may serve to remove some of the most elementary misunderstandings.

That fear in some form or other has played an essential part in God's dealings with men is evident from even a cursory reading of the inspired books of the Old Testament. The Old Law was given on Sinai in such a way as to instil terror into the hearts of the chosen people. "And all mount Sinai was on a smoke: because the Lord was come down upon it in fire, and the smoke arose from it as out of a furnace: and all the mount was terrible. And the sound of the trumpet grew by degrees louder and louder, and was drawn out to a greater length: Moses spoke and God answered him. And the Lord came down upon mount Sinai, in the very top of the mount, and He called Moses unto the top thereof. And when he was gone up thither, He said unto him: Go down and charge the people: lest they should have a mind to pass the limits to see the Lord, and a very great multitude of them should perish" (Exod. xix. 18–21). Time after time we read of the punishments God inflicted on His people when they proved unfaithful to the Law He had given them with such solemnity. There were defeats in battle, and captivities, and destruction of their towns and cities. In fact, it may be said that God led the Jews to keep the Law by fear of temporal loss and misery; and so true is this, that, as is evidenced by the book of Job, they had so far come to identify evil-doing with worldly failure and virtue with worldly prosperity that there were for them few problems of a more perplexing character than that of the undoubted success which seemed to crown the life of some of the bad and the misfortunes which awaited certain of the good—a state of affairs to which their understanding of Divine Providence gave no satisfying explanation.

St Paul in his epistles lays great stress on the fact that the New Law is the law of freedom and not of fear. "For you have not received the spirit of bondage again in fear . . ." (Rom. viii. 15). "So then, brethren, we are not the children of the bondwoman, but of the free: by the freedom wherewith Christ has made us free" (Gal. iv. 31). And this teaching of St Paul has been set in clear relief by the prince of theologians in the Iª IIᵃᵉ, QQ 106–108. In fact, we may venture to remark that it has been interpreted with a literalness and scrupulous faithfulness to the mind of the inspired writer which leads to conclusions that would appear hazardous were they not guaranteed by the authority of so great a theologian.

For St Thomas points out that the great difference between the Old Law and the New lies in this, that the Old Law was given by God principally in the tablets of stone which Moses carried from the mount. It was, then, something imposed on man from outside, and to the observance of which he was to be forced by the threat of punishment. But the New Law is given to us principally "in the fleshly tables of the heart" (2 Cor. iii. 3). The New Law is primarily the grace of the Holy Ghost, leading us sweetly and persuasively to do the will of Our Father. It is the law of freedom. Its source is within us—is the Holy Ghost enthroned in our hearts. We are not led by force, but march with joy in the way of the Lord, spurred on by the promptings of grace, animated by a thirst of the divine which leaves us no rest till it has been quenched at the wellsprings of the Godhead.

To some this may appear modernism. And this very fact should be reassuring. For what made, and makes, modernism attractive is the kernel of truth it contains. Modernism regards religion as a striving which rises spontaneously from the interior of man—the product of an unconscious urge to the Infinite. Modernism is false: it is the child of that human pride that wishes to make its own Gods. But it insists rightly on one truth: that our religion must be something vital: it must spring from within rather than adhere from without. Religion is the expression of a life, and life is always from within. No being could find happiness in turning towards God if it were not impelled to do so by a dictate of its own being. Were God entirely foreign to man man could find no peace in the possession of God. All this is true, and yet the modernist heresy can state much of what I have just said and still be wrong: for while we hold the vitality, the inwardness, of the religious instinct, we hold that it comes from God by grace and tends to a God outside us Who is the Author of that Grace. Our striving is to an objective God Who is not of our making; we strive in the power of His gratuitous gift; and even though that gift be really ours once we have received it, it remains none the less a gift. But if there be one point that we should in all conscience underline, it is that our striving is our own now; it springs from a principle that is in us and that is ours. We are now a law unto ourselves. For we have within our souls the grace of God which calls out for the possession of God, and carries us along with it in its passion for the Almighty.

We say that a man—a natural man, as yet not raised to the supernatural order—is free if he obeys the moral code. It is true that he follows a system of commands and prohibitions. There are certain restrictions imposed on him. There are things he may do and things he may not do. And yet we say that he is free: for the things that he may do are those to which his whole nature tends; the things which he may not do are those which tend ultimately to the destruction of his nature. In following the moral code he follows the dictates of his own nature and so is free. In transgressing it he submits himself to the world, or to passion, or to something else which is not his nature, and in doing so sacrifices his liberty, his power of being himself, in order to subject himself to the yoke of a principle lower than himself.

This explanation of liberty in the natural order would, of course, be accepted by most reasonable men. But there is a certain haziness in the matter of the freedom of the supernatural man. The natural man becomes a slave by submitting to principles lower than himself, it may be said. Is not then the supernatural man free in that he subjects himself to God—a principle higher than himself —and finds in submission to God freedom from all that is lower than God, including self?

Much might be said in defence of this conception of supernatural freedom. In fact I do not intend to refute it at all. It may be stated that it contains a truth, and a great truth. But it does violence to the commonly accepted idea of freedom, and, in addition, is included in the true concept of supernatural freedom, which I am about to explain. It needs, in other words, not refutation but explanation, it is not opposed to the true idea of freedom, but needs to be integrated into it.

Freedom in the natural man who submitted to the moral code arose from the fact that the code to which he submitted was but the formulation of the tendencies of his nature. Supernatural freedom also must mean that the New Law given us by God is not foreign to us, but is in its turn the expression of the tendencies of our "supernature". The New Law is but a formulation of the rules of conduct which development in spiritual stature involves. There is nothing forced about it, nothing enslaving. It is the law of our new spiritual being. To follow any other law is to become the slave of a system against which all that is of grace in us, and all that is of human nature, cries out with absolute decisiveness. To be united to God frees us then, because the soul in the state of grace wants God and can be kept from Him only by violence. We are free in going to God, because it is to Him that our whole being, raised by grace, tends to go. Our freedom is not, therefore, just a kind of mysterious freedom from all that is not God, without any explanation of why going to God is itself free. It is the freedom of obedience to an inward urge—the freedom of obeying a command that is really ours, of acting in accordance with a code written rather in our own hearts than in any collection of statutes and decrees.

That is why St Thomas makes the striking statement that "id quod est potissimum in lege novi testamenti, et in quo tota virtus ejus consistit, est gratia Spiritus Sancti, quae datur per fidem Christi; et ideo principaliter lex nova est ipsa gratia Spiritus Sancti, quae datur Christi fidelibus . . ." (I^a II^{ae}, Q 106)[1]. There is, of course, need for a written law, for guidance from the Church, the organ of the authority of Christ, her Head. But this is secondary in the eyes of St Thomas. The written law is but the expression of the law written in

---

[1] " . . . that which is of primary importance in the New Law, and in which all its driving power resides, is the grace of the Holy Ghost given through faith in Christ; and hence the New Law is before everything else, the grace of the Holy Ghost in Christ's faithful."

our souls by grace. We cannot read that law in all, or even in much of, its detail. Hence we have need of its being authoritatively proposed to us for our guidance—and this need is inescapable for man. But the written or spoken law adds nothing to the law of grace and the Holy Ghost. It is but a light to illumine the darkness that hides from us the truths imprinted deep within our innermost being.

If this be the true idea of the new dispensation, there are many who have failed to grasp its message. For fear, abject and perpetual, or half-resisted and inter-mittent, is too often a deciding factor in the lives of spiritual people. They live hemmed in by a fence of "don'ts". Were these prohibitions accepted as laws in the sense of dictates inspired by the nature of the end of man, and, on that account, to be followed not as impositions but as safeguards, there would be no question of slavery or bondage. But they are frequently not accepted in this spirit, and that very often for the good reason that they have no necessary connection at all with the end of man. Scrupulous people are the victims of a false concept of law which they obey under the compulsion of fear. They feel that the ego is endangered unless certain things be done, or avoided, and fearing above all else the possibility of harm to the ego, they follow blindly, and often in face of great suffering, the course of subjection to a rule which has no attraction for them, but which they deem it unsafe to disregard.

Even apart from cases of patent scrupulosity there are many others where fear enters to some extent. There are people who think that by omitting some practice to which they are attached, even if there be reason for omitting it, they have endangered their salvation, or, at any rate, have offended God. Fear is at the back of all this. They look on God as a tyrant who demands each day His pound of flesh and who will punish infallibly any irregularity whatever in the performance of the exterior act. There are people who, if they have been engaged in work for the glory of God during the whole day, and in accordance with the duties of their state, cannot bring themselves to go to bed at the appointed hour—even if it be appointed by their Rule—if on rare occasions they have found no free moment during the day to perform their usual exercises of piety. They think God would be displeased with them if they omitted one iota of the prescribed round of practices! They try to convince themselves that it is love of God, generosity in His service, that leads them to act thus; that it would be laziness to go to bed at the appointed hour if part of their ritual was still to be performed. They may even succeed in working themselves into good faith: at any rate, it is usually hard to work them around to any other state of mind, while saving them from laxity. But it is really fear that is at the back of their action. God is a tyrant. To save their souls they must at the close of every day be able to write "paid" to every promise they have made Him. And above all else—nothing must be left to the mercy and kindness of God. That would not be safe. It is far better to leave no loophole, to get through the round of devotions every day, no matter how unreasonable that may be; by so doing, salvation is made a certainty and there is no possibility of fear startling us with the dread thought that perhaps there is yet something to be done, something to be extorted. Such people are willing to give God everything except the one thing He wants— their confidence and their love. They want to make their future salvation a certainty even now through their own efforts; He wishes them to be saved by His mercy and nothing else. They fret and agitate themselves, are always in action, for fear gives them no rest; He wishes them to surrender themselves fully into His hands, to leave their salvation to His Omnipotence. What He asks is really more than they give—because He asks their all. But fear is too strong for them and they hold back from the greatest of all surrenders, fearing to believe that God is really a Father and wishes them to live as children in His house. Such souls know nothing of the freedom of the New Law. They are the slaves of a code imposed on them by fear.

"God hath not given us the spirit of fear: but of power, and of love, and of sobriety" (2 Tim. i. 7); and yet fear rules many lives, and in many different ways. There is, in the first place, a fear which leads us to desert God if we see that to follow Him will lead to suffering. This fear is opposed to the Holy Ghost. It is the fear of him who draws back from the open profession of his faith because he fears to lose his occupation—or of him, perhaps, who fears nothing more than the loss of a certain esteem he enjoyed before, or certain prospects of advancement in life. It is the fear of him who thinks that poverty is a real evil and who, sooner than risk poverty by being honest, thinks it preferable to rob the poor in trade. This fear makes slaves of free men. Their soul cries out for life, and they stifle its voice. All that is in them is opposed to the line of action that fear imposes. And so, they live in bondage; unable to free themselves from the fetters of fear; not daring to brave the illusory terrors of the world in order to win the real joys of heaven.

This fear, we have seen, is essentially bad, in that it leads us to lay greater store by the creature than by the Creator. And yet there is a fear of loss to self which may be the beginning of good. For God is able to inflict pain on man; and man can be brought to the service of God through the fear of punishment. We know by faith that sin deserves eternal damnation; that God is able and indeed has threatened to punish for all eternity those that defy His laws. Now man may be led to keep the law of God through love. But he may also be led to the same point by mere fear. And then he is once more a slave. The law of God is kept, but the soul has withdrawn itself from charity—if it ever had charity—and is therefore bound by a code to which it has no interior attraction. God is served in fear. His authority would be flouted had it nothing to commend it but its intrinsic majesty.

Were the soul to follow the dictates of its own corrupt being it would rise up against God. It is held in check by fear; it is the bondman of One Who is a Master and nothing more.

It should be noted that this fear, unlike that mentioned in the preceding paragraph, is not intrinsically bad. The first kind of fear—human or worldly respect— cannot but be bad, as it includes in itself the rejection of God. This second fear includes necessarily only the fear of the divine punishment. If this fear be present in a soul that does not love, it has the defect of servility to which reference has been made. It may, however, remain on in the soul even when love has entered and then it becomes subordinated to love; we fear God's wrath, but we love Him also; and the fear of punishment becomes an incentive to greater love. This is the fear of beginners in the spiritual life. It is not bad; it is merely imperfect. When perfect love comes into the soul it has the effect of casting out fear as a motive force.

"Fear is not in charity: but perfect charity casteth out fear, because fear hath pain; And he that feareth is not perfected in charity" (John iv. 18).

The beginner has often been brought to a realization of the existence of a spiritual order by the conviction that God can and will punish evildoing for all eternity. "For all eternity"—the very words inspire terror. The reason is the same as that which accounts for the import- ance the idea of God as Creator may have at the same stage of spiritual development. Nothing less than a startling—and at first glance unpleasant—truth is sufficient to waken us out of our torpor. There are few people who will be so penetrated at the beginning of their spiritual lives by the thought that God loves them, that nothing more will be required to effect in them a conversion of a radical nature. Men are led by the thirst for pleasure, and nothing is more likely to draw them from the pursuit of unlawful pleasure than the threat of very real pain. Only in rare circumstances will the realization that there is a higher, a divine, pleasure come home to them with enough force to draw them from the mode of life which is actually affording them a degree of satisfaction that experience has not yet shown to be incomplete. Man at the beginning must rather be turned Godwards, than move thither of himself. And the great turning forces are awe and fear.

If it be true that fear usually plays so great a part in the beginnings of a conversion, it follows that even as the soul advances the element of fear will be eliminated only gradually. Fear has worked its way into the soul's psychological make-up. It has possibly been for a time the determining factor in its outlook on life. Love follows; but it finds a master in possession of the soul, who may be supplanted slowly, but whose hand is so firmly on the controls that there can be no question, in normal circumstances, of its being ousted from the very start. And so it happens that love reigns in the soul—

but fear is ever by her side. At times the act of love predominates; at times it is the act of fear that is most in evidence. But love grows. Fear recedes ever into the background. The time comes when, even if we still fear the pain of hell, and act under the coercion of this fear, we love God more than hell is feared, and the thought of losing Him Whom we love is harder to bear than even the thought of the suffering He might inflict. Love has begun to take effective command. Fear becomes more and more the servant of love. Fear, which before disputed the throne, is now admitted only as a slave. Love uses man's natural fear of punishment to spur him on, though all unwillingly, to a more radical renouncement of this world. Love, one might almost say, plays with fear. It panders to its weakness, but only in order to obtain an end that belongs not to fear but to love. Man's fear for self is used to make him give up self; his dread of suffering is made an excuse for inviting him to nail himself to the cross.

"Perfect charity," St John has told us, "casteth out fear." Will no fear remain when love will be master? What then happens to the gift of Fear? Is it only for a time? Must it, too, be cast out, allowing man to stand utterly unabashed in the presence of the Divine Majesty?

We have so far mentioned three kinds of fear. But none of these was the Fear which is a gift of the Holy Ghost, though the fear of the beginner in charity, of which we have just spoken, includes the Fear which is a gift. The fear of the beginner is, in fact, a complex of servile and childlike fear, for the precise reason that it is a complex of slavery and of the freedom of charity. The time has, however, now come to speak of childlike fear—that is to say, the Fear that is a gift—remembering always that it enters, concomitantly with charity, of which it is the fruit, into the spiritual state of the beginner who is actually in the state of grace.

The object of all fear is impending evil. If the evil feared be the chastisement which God may inflict, the fear is that of beginners, or of slaves. But there is something that may be feared more than any chastisement, something that can strike the soul as being an evil in a far more radical way than any physical pain, and that is the deprivation of something that is loved, something that is the whole aim of life. Now God is what the soul who is ruled by charity loves and desires above everything else. Such a soul has a burning thirst for God. Its days are days of waiting till the star will rise and the glory of the Lord will be revealed in it. Nothing, therefore, is really an evil in its eyes compared with the loss of God. And God, it sees, can be lost only by its own sin, only through its own fault. For it the great evil is sin, for by sin it may lose God. It fears to offend God, not so much because He will punish the offence, but because sin will result in the loss of Him Whom the heart desires. Such a soul lives in a state of chaste and holy fear: chaste, for it is a fear untainted by the world; holy, for it is a fear that has its source in God.

It seems strange at the first glance to find a gift, Fear, entering into the domain of a theological virtue, Hope, and, what is still more unexpected, opposing itself to it. For Hope also regulates our attitude to the attaining of the vision of God, and it gives us the power to have confidence that the uninterrupted contemplation of the Divine Essence will one day be ours. Fear, on the contrary, concentrates on the possibility of failing in our final end, and replaces confidence by a deep-rooted sense of mistrust. How can this be? Can God really have intended to fill us with such conflicting feelings?

The opposition here suggested between hope and fear is most fruitful for the clear understanding of the nature of the latter. Hope has as object the life of glory in heaven attainable through the divine Omnipotence. But, though it be God Who works in us both to will and to accomplish, we also work under Him. Our salvation is, therefore, the work of two; of God and of man; and the soul may fear failure through the defection of either the one or the other. The soul considered from the side of its native power is utterly incapable of ever seeing God. It cannot then put its hope of seeing Him in itself. There is only God Who can be the secure basis of such a hope. And it is the theological virtue known by the name of Hope— and being, hence, hope *par excellence*—which enables us to turn trustfully to the divine Omnipotence, knowing that it can give what we are powerless to obtain.

Hope, therefore, gives us the assurance that we can see God. Charity makes us want to see Him. Hope alone without charity cannot give rise to holy fear; for to lose what one does not seek is not regarded as an evil. But once charity takes possession of the soul nothing is of so great importance as to see God. Hope tells us that with His help we can see Him. But there still remains that other factor in the working out of human destiny— the individual himself, with all his weakness, with all his bias towards what is evil. Here is a factor that may lead to the loss of God. God will not fail us; but we may fail Him. Were our salvation the work of God alone, there would be no need for more than Hope. But salvation is the work of man as well; and where man is found there will be failure and fear.

The gift of Fear—it follows—is not opposed to Hope. It is its necessary complement. Hope relies on the divine Omnipotence; Fear doubts human frailty. Hope is confident that salvation is possible with God's help; fear realizes that man may oppose himself to God and so frustrate the designs of the Most High. Hope rises joyously in the strength of the Almighty; and the soul that fears is borne aloft with Hope, trembling at the thought that her nothingness has the power to resist the All that holds her in His mighty grasp.

Our fear—even the Fear which is a gift of the Holy Ghost—consists in this attitude of reverence in the presence of that Almighty Power with which we may find ourselves in conflict, and of that Good which we may lose without hope of recovery. It comprises two elements, reverence for God, and flight from impending evil. We revere the Person of Him in Whose hands we are, Who has complete and absolute ownership of our being, Whose infinity is raised so far above our pigmy stature. It is a flight from evil—from the possible loss of God. And God may be lost—through our own fault as long as we remain pilgrims in this vale of tears. Fear will, on this account, remain a driving force for the whole of our lives. But it will be a real driving force, not a paralysing restraint. For it will lead us to confide our nothingness entirely to God. Our nothingness may lead to failure. The goal of love is God's for the giving. Let us offer everything up to the Omnipotent—weakness, frailty, and all—offer all to Him that He may be all in all, that it be His strength alone that bears our burden, and that His Pity be awakened by our all too patent need.

For the sake of completeness it is well to note that the necessity of a gift of Fear may be seen if we consider—as we have done throughout this book—the fact that our sonship by grace is merely adoptive. We have seen the need of the adopted child for intellectual guidance, for strength and childlike devotion. There is, as well, a need of fear. For fear is the antidote to presumption, and there is always a real danger that an adopted child, after the first few days of awkwardness, may grow into an attitude of easy familiarity, and blind self-confidence, which will bar all possibility of its ever submitting to the discipline of training. It can, thus, have hope to the extent of presumption, and this not in the goodness of its new father, but in its own power to do and to advance. It has forgotten its own limitations, that it has need of a gratuitous re-education; and it not infrequently happens that its insupportable arrogance leads to its being disowned by the father whose kindness it has done nothing to repay. We are such children, admitted into the family of God Himself. We must never cease to remember that it is His grace and mercy that have admitted us; that of ourselves we can contribute only spiritual boorishness. Reverence and fear are then becoming in us. We are allowed to be the children of God; what thought should be more present to the mind than that of our unworthiness?

"Blessed are the poor in spirit: for theirs is the kingdom of heaven" (Matt. v. 3). The poor in spirit are they who fear the Lord. They know their nothingness and accept it, confiding it to Him Who is omnipotent. They fear but one evil: to offend God, and by offending Him to lose Him. But their offence can come from no source other than themselves. And having given all that they are to the keeping of their Father, they know that their steps will not falter in the way and that they will see God. Blessed are they for they have learned to unite into the synthesis of love, trust in God and distrust of self—the freedom of the child of God and the reverence of the creature. Their lives are all one piece, and the pattern is love; the voices of all the virtues rise from their lips to God, and the voices blend into a poem of praise, for it is the Holy Spirit that sings in them. The Holy Spirit and His love light up their hearts, and the narrow way shows smooth and soft to tread.

The Fear which is a gift of the Holy Ghost is, then, the fear of losing God, the child's fear of being separated from its father. To be ruled by this fear is to be free, not to be enslaved. For it is a fear that is rooted in love. It is the fear of losing the One Good that we desire, the One Good to which we are drawn by the weight of the grace that is in us. It is a fear that leads us to treasure our freedom and use it only to attain what we really will. The fear of creatures, the fear of pain, enslave. They force the will to bend itself to their dictates, and thereby it ceases to be master of itself. The fear of the world is always bad; for the will can never bound its longings by the limits of the created. The fear of pain may be turned to good and made the tool of freedom, if it submit to be diverted into the channels that the will traces. But the Fear of God is always good, always sets us free. For it is the snapping of the last cord that checks our ardent flight to God—self, namely. Fear frees us from self, and self is the last obstacle to union with Our Father. Fear teaches us that self can be but a hindrance, that it can lead to losing God; and thus it is that fear leads us by another path to the very goal which is the goal of love—total and entire donation of all that we are to God Our Father in heaven. "O how great is the multitude of the sweetness, O Lord, which Thou hast hidden for them that fear Thee!" (Ps. xxx. 20).

CHAPTER IX

THE BEATITUDES

"Blessed are they that dwell in thy house, O Lord." (Ps. lxxxiii. 5)

It must never be forgotten when speaking of the gifts of the Holy Ghost that they are infused into the soul directly by God Himself, and can be obtained no other way. Though they are habits they differ from the natural or acquired habits in that they cannot be caused by our repeated acts. A person may acquire the natural virtue of bravery by acting bravely. By repeated efforts to overcome timidity, or to restrain foolhardiness, as the case may be, he succeeds at length in acquiring mastery over the movements of the combative part of his soul. This mastery is true courage or the virtue of Fortitude. But only God can cause the gifts, including, evidently, the gift of Fortitude. For the gifts being special powers of submitting ourselves to the divine guidance can be caused in us by Him alone Who is to be the guide. The natural virtues have as end to bring all that there is in man under the control of reason. It is consequently but to be expected that they should be caused under the dictation of the reason they are destined to obey. In quite similar manner the gifts are caused by Him Who is to move them, namely God Himself. And just as it is He alone Who directs their activity when we have them, it is He alone Who can give them to us when we lack them.

It might seem to follow from the fact that we cannot by our own unaided efforts acquire the gifts, that time spent in thinking of them or in reading about them is simply wasted. It is clearly a good thing to read about brave deeds, since to become brave it is sufficient to imitate the deeds of which we have just read. But to acquire the courage which is a gift, repetition of acts is worthless. In fact, unless we have the gift already we cannot produce a single act having in it even the germ of that courage which the Holy Ghost gives. In spite of this, however, it is a good, even a very good, thing to consider the doctrine of the gifts; and that for various reasons.

In the first place, to know them is to conceive the desire of having them. The natural consequence of knowing them should be to turn in humble prayer to the Holy Ghost Whose gifts they are that He may deign to pour them into our souls. He Who is Love, and Who desires our full sanctification, will hear this prayer and will use His gifts to work in us the plans of God's mercy.

In the second place meditation on the gifts leads us to see how far we have still to go in the ways of perfection, how much there is in us that is not yet God's, and what we may yet become with the help of grace. The gifts reveal to us a state of soul in which God is everything. God alone is seen in the world, for the world is seen in God. It is the strength of God that wages the battle of life. It is the wisdom of God that unlocks the mysteries of life. It is the absence of God that is the great tragedy of life. And we learn that this concentration of life on God is not to be the exclusive right of a few souls. It is intended to be the normal condition of every soul in the state of grace. For every such soul is the child of its Eternal Father and has received the gifts in order to enable it to live on the plane of its new dignity.

It is at times easy to say that the level of sanctity of any particular saint is not for us—and this in spite of that fact that Our Lord Himself sets us a still higher standard in telling us to be perfect as our Heavenly Father is perfect. But no one can say that the holiness of the gifts is not for him. He has the gifts in his soul and the Holy Ghost is ready to lead him by their means. The gifts are not something optional. It is the doctrine of St Thomas that they are necessary for salvation. To withdraw oneself from the influence of the gifts is to withdraw oneself from a necessary means of saving one's soul.

It is the gifts that effect our final sanctification. It is by their means that we submit ourselves fully to the action of God in our souls. This is a thought that leads to complete abandonment of self to our Heavenly Father. For our sanctification is seen, under a new head, to be not our work but the work of God. It is from Him that all grace comes. But as the crown and perfection of every grace, we stand in need of the grace of the gifts, and that, that we may become all that God wants us to be. Holiness, true holiness, is the work of the gifts, and the gifts are the work of God and of Him alone. We can do but one thing: we can submit to the action of God; we can pray and hold ourselves in readiness. We must become empty of self, that God may enter. And when after years of prayer and tears grace will have begun to flower in our souls, and we shall know that the seeding time of eternity cannot be long to wait, we shall have the unutterable and ravishing joy of knowing that all that is in us, sin and evil only excepted, has been the gift of the divine Love; that we are a little corner of the universe where God has begun to reign in undisputed sway.

It follows from what has just been said that the gifts are due to the operation of God alone in our souls and that the most that we can do is to pray that He may give them to us, and to dispose ourselves for them by a practical realization of our helplessness and need of divine assistance. But though our part may seem to be small, we should have no doubt that the gifts will be given us if we do what is required of us. For they are the gifts of the Holy Spirit who is Love. God loves us and wishes to load us with favours. This is the great mystery of God's relations with His rational creatures. Already in creating them He had been unspeakably generous. For in doing so He drew them out of nothing and gave them their whole being with all its perfections. Not content with this, however, He decided to allow His love to lavish upon them the greatest of all gifts that can be made to a mere creature—the gift of a share in His own life. It was love that led God to this decision —His boundless desire to give to others a share in the fulness that was in Himself. And His love leads Him to take every means that His Wisdom suggests for the attainment of this end. Such a means are the gifts of the Holy Ghost, the gifts of divine love. They are destined to make us enter more fully into the life of grace and so to come to an ever greater degree of nearness to and intimacy with God for all eternity. It is then the selfsame Love which prompted God to invite us to a share in His own Life and which prompted Him to offer us His gifts. One offering is as absolute as the other. As surely as God wishes us to see Him and love Him for all eternity so surely does He wish to submit us to the guidance of the gifts. The gifts are a means—and an essential means—to the end He wills, namely our salvation. And willing the end He is bound to will the means without which the end cannot be attained.

It follows from this that the gifts, being the means adopted by Divine Love to lead us to union with God, are attributed to the Holy Ghost Who is Subsistent Love. The same conclusion is arrived at if we consider that the Holy Ghost is Subsistent Holiness.   In the cycle of the Blessed Trinity the Holy Ghost proceeds from the Father and the Son by way of Love. The Father and Son, seeing in Each other the marvellous beauty of the Godhead, are united in an embrace of love whence proceeds the Holy Ghost. The Holy Ghost is then the expression of the Father's attachment to the Son and the Son's attachment to the Father, and on this account is said to be Holy, for holiness in God is simply God's identity with and inseparability from His own Perfection. Nothing defiled can enter God. For God is Purity. God is Perfection. God is so fixed in His attachment to Himself that He would cease to be God were He to deviate from the norm of being and action which is His Own Essence. It has, however, been pointed out that one of the consequences of the gifts of the Holy Ghost is to free us from things of earth that we may be more closely united to God. Therefore, since our holiness consists in adhering to the God of all holiness and purity, and in freedom from every stain opposed to God, the effect of the gifts may aptly be considered as holiness, and hence to be appropriated to the Spirit of Holiness, the Holy Ghost.

Scholastic theologians in speaking of holiness point out that the Greek word for "holy" means properly, "not of earth", or "not tainted by earth". The gifts free us from the earth. They purify our vision and our judgment. They free us from doubt in action. They teach us to despise the strength that is of this world and to act in the strength of God. They wean us from service of creatures and consecrate us to the service of Our Father in heaven. They tell us that the only evil is to lose God; that the world is to be despised and counted as trash that God be gained. And in making us not of this world they make us other-worldly, they attach us to God. The gifts, in other words, make us holy in both a positive and a negative sense; holy in the sense of being freed from all that is not God, all that is defiled, and holy in the sense of possessing That Which alone is pure. It is but natural on this account to consider them as the special gift of that Divine Person Who is called Holy, even though they be the gift of all Three Persons. For this is the essence of appropriation—to attribute to One of the Divine Persons, because of some special similarity to His Person and Attributes, an operation common to all Three.

There remains still one reason why the gifts should be appropriated to the Holy Ghost and that is that He is a Spirit—that He is called the Holy Spirit. Spirit means breath; and the Holy Ghost is the Subsistent Breath of the Divine Love. Father and Son, united in Their embrace of Love, breathe forth the Holy Spirit, the token and expression of Their mutual love. Now, the idea of a breath suggests a strong, yet gentle, impulse. It calls to our minds a soft ocean breeze, bellying a vessel's sails and urging it irresistibly and persuasively to port. The gifts are the sails of our soul; and God breathes into them that we may come to our eternal haven. But it is the Holy Spirit Who is the Breath of the Trinity. Therefore, it is He Who is said to guide and impel us by the gifts. The gifts impel us: they are the gifts of Love. He Who is Spirit and Holy and Love is the Holy

Ghost. The gifts are then His. They are the gifts of the Holy Ghost.

The idea that the gifts are God's means for bringing us to the goal of love, namely our eternal beatitude suggests another which theology has not been slow to develop: that there is a relation between the gifts and the beatitudes of which Our Lord spoke during His sermon on the mount. We know that perfect happiness will be ours only in the next world. Perfect happiness consists in the face to face vision and in the love of God. But while we remain on earth we cannot see God face to face. Our desires will, therefore, never be satiated on earth. There will be always something greater to await. Our hearts were made for God and while we wander far from Him in this vale of tears they will find no lasting rest. Our greatest joy must be in love and hope; love of Him Whom we do not see, buoyed up by the hope of seeing Him when our journeying will have reached its term. But though perfect happiness is impossible without the clear vision of the goal of happiness, God, there is a measure of happiness and content that can be ours even in this world. We can arrive at a mode of life and activity yielding deep peace and joy, providing, in fact, a resting place on the road to heaven where the soul may pause, knowing that it is tasting in some small way the joy that awaits it in eternity. There is a beatitude of this world just as there is a beatitude of heaven. The beatitude of the wayfarer is, it is true, but a certain anticipation, a certain foretaste, of what that of God's guest will be. But it is a real beatitude, a real goal, a real haven of rest and peace in the midst of toil and pain. God has been so good as to grant that even our way of life be lit up by flashes of the glory that lights the courts of heaven; and from time to time our ears of clay hear echoes of that music that swells and rings in heaven's halls.

It was this that Our Lord had in mind when He repeated again and again: "Blessed are . . ." There are, He tells us, even here on earth, certain people who have begun to taste of the joy of heaven. Such are indeed blessed. And doubly so. For not only are they blessed in what they have in this life, but the earthly blessedness is a guarantee of one that is yet to come. They are blessed in the hope as well as in reality. In serving and loving God they have found the secret all men seek to find—the secret of happiness. And the answer to their quest has not been, as it could have been: "Time is for suffering; eternity is long enough for rejoicing," but it has been that there is a joy in the pain of earth and that that joy is sweet as is the joy of heaven.

"Blessed are the poor in spirit: for theirs is the kingdom of heaven." This is the first of the beatitudes—it is the first of those states or actions in which Our Lord tells us that true happiness consists. Poverty of spirit, like every other beatitude, is not the effect of one gift alone. But it is convenient—and it has been approved by the practice of Doctors and Theologians—to consider each beatitude as corresponding to a single gift; or, at least, to some only of the gifts. This should be borne in mind when reading the following lines. When it is said that poverty of spirit is the fruit of Fear of the Lord it is not meant thereby to exclude the possibility of Wisdom, for example, leading to the same result. All that is intended is that Fear will certainly lead there in the way attributed to it, while the question whether there be another way through the practice of acts of another gift is left to the personal enquiry of the reader.

"Blessed are the poor in spirit." The gift of Fear leads to poverty of spirit. Fear is distrust of self, realization that failure is possible if there be no strength to count on but our own. And so Fear leads to humility, and humility is the food of Fear. Knowing what is in man we look on ourselves as poor, as nothingness. Our riches, our talents, make no difference. The poverty of the beatitude is not the poverty of destitution. It is the spiritual poverty of those who have denuded themselves of self. It is poverty of spirit. It is the antithesis of pride of life. Pride of life consists in that feeling of being something, of being a force in the world, of being a power to be reckoned with even if the struggle be a spiritual one. This pride is the pride of him who is conscious, but falsely, of his power, and who glories in his riches of strength and worth. The fallen angels who refused to serve had this pride. They experienced the full value of the gift of being and life that God had given them, and shutting their eyes to the fact that it came from God they dared to measure themselves against Him. Ordinary souls are not tempted as were these spirits. But still, every attempt to live life in one's own strength is to measure oneself against God. For life is a spiritual conflict into which God enters. There are Divine forces at play in human life, and the goal of life is a share in the life of God Himself. To try to live without God's aid is to repeat the sin of the fallen angels in a human way, and being doomed to failure it carries even in itself the bitterness and hollowness of the impending catastrophe. The poor in spirit, on the other hand, experience even now the joy that will be theirs, when the kingdom of heaven will harbour them. For even now they act in the power of God. Acting in His power they have a spiritual awareness of the necessity of their triumph. They know that heaven will be theirs. Though they have no strength of their own to force an entry, though they have no riches of their own to purchase a share in its joy, they know that it will be theirs through the riches and bounty of Him Who reigns there, and fear of their own weakness is lost in joy at the strength of God.

"Blessed are the meek: for they shall possess the land." It is usual to consider courage as opposed to cowardice and to that alone. By doing so the essentially vicious nature of foolhardiness and brutality tends to be forgotten, whereas it is precisely the gift of Fortitude, which is the gift of spiritual courage, that leads to meekness. The reason is very similar to that we have just seen when speaking of poverty of spirit. Fortitude is the gift which enables us to combat in the power of God. The power of God, however, is not destructive. God's power is tempered by sweetness and mercy. His strength seems but gentleness. To act in the power of God is then to act with gentle persuasiveness. There will be no doubt about eventual success—that is to say in the attainment of what is really the goal; for though the will of God will certainly be accomplished, perhaps this may not be in the way which we had envisaged. But there will be no overpowering brutality, no disregard for others' pain. To urge one's views in face of unnecessary pain and anguish is a confession of weakness. It is to confess that one's purpose is of such ephemeral and narrow scope that it is indissolubly linked up with the success or failure of life's material minutiae. The man of God has a wider, a universal purpose. He can reach his end—the Will of His Father—even when he seems to fail in the world's eyes, even when he lays aside in mercy and compassion what zeal had led him to undertake, and having a transcendant purpose he has a strength to match. It is not weakness that prompts him to withdraw when to do so appears to the world to be an admission of failure. It is rather disciplined strength that is his motive force. He has restrained his hand from the quest of earthly glory, but heaven is in his grasp. A little while of waiting and he will enter a victor—sharing in the triumph of his victor King Who entered glorious into His Kingdom on the first Ascension Thursday—into the joy that the might of his arm and the strength of his restrains have won. He has been meek—but it is he who will possess the promised land. And from time to time he sees, as it were, the magic of its hills show faint beyond earth's horizon; and then is he truly blessed, for he sees his own home.

"Blessed are they that mourn for they shall be comforted." The gift of Knowledge is, as we have seen already, the gift of mourning. Knowledge is the gift that enables us to judge rightly in terms of created realities. And we saw that in our pre-occupation with the created, no idea could come home to us with greater force than that of the essentially transitory character of all that is not God. Knowledge tells us that we live in a world that will pass; that the beauty of the world will fade; that friends will die; that health will fail and eyes grow dim. The soul is inundated with sorrow, for it sees but death and disillusionment. Where can be the blessedness of this deep and bitter grief? It is concealed in love. Knowledge, like every other gift, is the child of charity. If it tells us that the world is nothingness, it is because it is so that God sees it, and because He Whom we love is far above the pettiness of what we lose. We shall weep at our loss but be comforted by our gain. It is God Himself Who wipes the tears from our eyes. As yet we cannot say that mourning and grief will be no more. But there will be consolation: there will be the balm of love. There will be the blessedness of mourning when comfort is at hand, and when comfort is given in terms of love.

"Blessed are they that hunger and thirst after justice; for they shall have their fill." To hunger and thirst after justice is to devote oneself without reserve to the service of God: It is, in other words, to be under the sway of the gift of Piety. Piety sees that God is our Father, and leads us to devote ourselves to Him in the spirit of childlike self-oblivion. The right comes to be regarded no longer as merely what should be done; it is now a way of serving a loving Father. It is not done by constraint; it becomes a passion, an insatiable hunger and thirst. No loving child bargains when there is a question of serving its parents. It would be uneasy if it were selfish in the slightest way. Piety is just this unselfishness in the service of God. It is a hunger and thirst after the things that please a Father. And it finds its fill in that Father's good pleasure. The selfless son delights in the joy that his father experiences in the services rendered to him. Piety teaches us to rejoice in having given all to our Father in Heaven. It is, then, the fount and spring of a beatitude, and, as such, it is a foretaste of heaven.

"Blessed are the merciful; for they shall obtain mercy." This beatitude is one which confirms the statement made earlier to the effect that each beatitude was not the fruit of just one gift, but that many might be operative in its production. For it is clear that Fortitude, in so far as it means disciplined strength, is at play in mercy. And again it is Piety that leads us to treat kindly those who are the children of our heavenly Father.

St Thomas, however, following St Augustine, sees in this beatitude a special intervention of the gift of Counsel —though St Thomas for his part is careful to explain that the role he attributes to it is not exclusive of the other gifts. He gives as reason that mercy has been in a special way recommended to us by Almighty God —it is in other words, His special counsel to us—and should then be in a particular manner the fruit of the gift which enables us to follow the interior advice of the Holy Ghost, namely the gift of Counsel. He quotes in support of his contention the text wherein the prophet Daniel recommends almsgiving to King Nabuchodonosor as a means of placating the Divine wrath: "Wherefore O King, let my counsel be acceptable to thee, and redeem thou thy sins with alms, and thy iniquities with works of mercy to the poor; perhaps he will forgive thy offences" (Dan. iv. 24).

This special association of mercy with counsel seems at first sight to be quite arbitrary since Almighty God counsels the practice of all the gifts and virtues. St Thomas, one would be tempted to say, had to link mercy up with something and found an excuse for making counsel that something in the convenient text of the Book of Daniel. To say this is, of course, to attribute modern intellectual slovenliness to a mind that sought truth and could not tolerate the pleasant jingle of catch-phrases. For this reason alone it is indefensible. But there is in addition one other very good reason, and that is that there is really a closer connection between mercy and counsel than appears to the superficial observer, and that St Thomas really stated a profound truth when he seemed to be indulging in verbiage. For there is hardly any virtue which needs more to be the object of a special divine recommendation than that of mercy, since there is hardly any other which appeals less to this world. Why, considering the matter from the point of view of the world, should one show mercy to the poor, to enemies? Why should one waste one's own substance in keeping the breath of life in shiftless individuals whose reaction to almsgiving may even be abuse of the alms and importunate worrying of the almsgiver? The law of the world is the law of the jungle. The poor and weak are life's failures. The sooner they admit it the better for all concerned. Why should a man endanger his own chances of success by hanging around his neck the dead weight of the wretched that cling to him and sap his strength and riches? To do so would be sheer folly and yet—to do so is what God wishes of us. God saw that this truth would never dawn on man if man were left to himself. Did not St Paul, when in inspired words he described the godless as ". . . without affection, without fidelity, without mercy" (Rom. i. 31), intend to sketch in few words what man is without God? Man needed the living example of One Who would be meek and humble of heart, Who would not crush the bruised reed nor extinguish the smoking flax, Who would have pity on the multitude that was as sheep without a shepherd—man needed all that to convince him that mercy was something noble, that worth and character could be shown as clearly in the readiness to aid a fallen foe as in the determination to avenge a slighting word. On that account mercy is pre-eminently a matter of divine counsel and flows in a particularly intimate manner from Counsel the gift.

"Blessed are the merciful; for they shall obtain mercy." True happiness is found in the possession of God; the true happiness of this earth is in the secure hope that God will one day be ours. This latter happiness is that of the

merciful. "For all have sinned and do need the glory
of God" says St Paul (Rom. iii. 23). No man can believe
sincerely that he deserves heaven as a reward for the
eked-out paltriness of his life. Heaven, if ever we are
received there, will be opened to us by the mercy of our
Gentle Redeemer. To know the quality of this mercy
one must have been merciful too. If a man has ever felt
his heart go out to misery and has given his heart free
rein, then, and only then, has he some idea of God's
compassion and mercy. If we cannot resist the cry of
the need of others, how can God resist ours? If we,
who, after all, are only fellow wayfarers with our brethren,
if we cannot close our ears to their prayers without
feeling the shame of having degraded our persons to the
level of the brute beasts, what must be the tenderness
and solicitude of Him Who died to save all of our souls?
Blessed are the merciful for they shall obtain that of
which they stand in inescapable need—the mercy of
Omnipotence, the power of the All-merciful. Blessed
are they that are led by the counsel of the Spirit of Love,
for God is love and he that abideth in love abideth in
God.

The ninth beatitude—the last we shall consider in this
present chapter—corresponds to the gift of Understanding.
"Blessed are the clean of heart; for they shall see God."
Faith is perfected by understanding, which draws back
in some way the veil of obscurity behind which God is
concealed from eyes of flesh. In heaven faith will be
no more and understanding will have merged itself in
vision. The clean of heart—they that have crucified their
flesh with the vices and concupiscences—see God in
understanding. They have realized that it is sin in them
that obscures vision. God is everywhere, but the pure
alone see the God of purity. God is a spirit, God is not

of this world: to see Him the eye must be spiritualized and the heart must be swept clean of earthly stains. If the pain of this process be borne, blessedness will result; for God will be seen. He will not be seen face to face as yet; He will be seen but indistinctly, will be glimpsed and sensed, rather than unveiled. It will be God Himself, however, with Whom we shall be in contact. He, on Whom the Angels fear to gaze, will be close to us: we shall know that He is there as a Friend, that He is there awaiting the hour of the great appointment. Pain, anxiety, unease, will be no more. In their place will be the blessedness of a dawn that speaks of the full noon-day.

CHAPTER X

BROTHERS OF CHRIST

"Blessed are the peacemakers: for they shall be called the children of God." (Matt. v. 9)

There remain still two beatitudes to be considered. In treating of them we shall not follow the Gospel order, since the one which comes second in the order of their enumeration by St Matthew is the one that will be considered first. This beatitude comes eighth in the complete list. "Blessed are they that suffer persecution for justice' sake: for theirs is the kingdom of heaven."

It is perhaps not far-fetched to hear in this beatitude an echo of the words in which Our Lord tells us that the kingdom of heaven suffereth violence and that the violent bear it away: or of those other no less striking words in which He invites us to take up our cross if we desire to have a share with Him. For the eighth beatitude is a statement of the general principle that the world hates them that are not of the world; and that they who cleave to God will find themselves at war with all that is not God. The cross, in some shape, is an inevitable companion of godliness when godliness is engrafted on to a fallen nature and when it is to develop in surroundings that are inimical to its principles. The cross in our lives is then the test of our godliness. If the cross be totally absent we are not of God. If the cross be present there is every reason to believe that we are living over again in our lives Him Who was God and suffering Man. The cross, persecution, is a guarantee that we are on the right path.

The cross will take various forms. At the beginning of our spiritual lives it will be but light and easily recognizable as something heaven-sent. Later on it will be harder to feel that what we endure is a cross. There will be suffering. But its supernatural and beneficent character will be hidden from us. We shall be obliged to view our cross with eyes of faith, or else fail to recognize in it the familiar outlines of God's chosen instrument of purification. But it will be all the more the cross on that account. God will have begun to purify spirit as well as sense. And in the midst of pain and aridity there will be deep down in the interior of our souls the calm assurance that God is with us. Our suffering will, in some sublime way, guarantee His presence. The cross has its own way of revealing itself to the soul; the cross has its own spiritual fragrance by which it may be known. The cross will then be our reason for believing that we possess God. The joy of knowing that the kingdom of heaven is ours will be occasioned by the fact of there being persecution to suffer and justice to follow in pain and anguish.

We may on this account agree with St Thomas in considering the eighth beatitude as referring not to any one gift in particular, but as implying a certain perfection in the working of all the gifts, whereby man is enabled to pursue justice in the face of opposition and even persecution. And it is a consoling thought that Our Lord has promised a special share of His own joy here on earth to those who suffer for Him. Each gift has its own joy attached to it. But there is, in addition, a special joy to be found in the exercise of the gifts when that exercise costs. God has really made the way to heaven easy for those who advance along it without reserve and guided by the Holy Spirit. Even suffering becomes for them the occasion of joy.

It is, however, of the seventh beatitude that I intend to speak in most detail in this, the last chapter of this little book. "Blessed are the peacemakers: for they shall be called the children of God." There are many reasons why this beatitude should be singled out for special treatment.

In the first place, it is the only beatitude which refers explicitly to the fact of being the child of God. We had seen that it was our adoptive childhood through grace that necessitated the gifts. Would it not seem then to follow that the beatitude which is most directly brought into relation with childhood through grace must stand in a peculiar relation to the gifts also? Then there is the intriguing reference to the "peacemaker". What can there be in the peacemaker that he should be singled out for the greatest of all joys—that of being the child of God? Besides we know that all our perfection consists in our resemblance to Christ, Our Head. He is the Son of God by nature. It is to Him more than to anyone else that the term "child of God" can be applied. Is it possible that there is some hidden connection between Our Lord and peacemakers such that the peacemakers imitate Him in an extremely distinctive manner and are thereby entitled to be called the children of God *par excellence*?

To answer the last query first, we may state that it is unquestionably true that the character of Our Lord may be summed up in the term "peacemaker". The angelic choir sang on the night of His birth: "And on earth peace to men of good will". He was the Peacemaker Who made peace. He did not just settle quarrels between man and man; He came to harmonize all that jarred in God's creation, all that had withdrawn itself outside the tranquillity of order. He came to make peace, in that He came to restore beauty and order to what sin had dismembered. Where sin had set up enmities He would establish concord. Isaias spoke of Our Lord as the "Prince of peace". We read in the Roman Martyrology that the time of Our Lord's birth was a time of peace. This fact has been singled out by the Church for mention in her Martyrology in preference to so many others that might have been selected because it was felt that there was a divine purpose in the coincidence of peace and the birth of the Prince of peace. And then does not St Paul—as he so often does—epitomize revelation in that striking phrase: "For He is our peace" (Eph. ii. 14)? Christ not only brought peace; He *is* peace; He is *our* peace. In Him is the harmony of all that wars and strives.

He is our peace, for He is our peace with the Father. Man had offended God by sin. The sin of Adam was the sin of the human race, committed even in his official capacity as head. Sin is an offence against God, a turning away from God. But to offend God is to cause God to turn away from a sinner. And so the effect of sin is enmity. Man is turned away from God to earth, and God, offended and outraged in His sovereign rights, is turned away from man. Friendship is a state of mutual love and affection based on community of life and interests. But between God and the sinner there is held in common neither life nor interests. To sin grievously is to turn from the life that is of God to the death that is of the world; it is to dethrone God from the centre of our thoughts and to set up in His place the idol of self, the idol of pleasure, the idol of power. The sinner has within himself a principle of death. He will perish as will the vanities on which he founded his hope. His interests are centred far from God. Having thus neither life nor interest in common with God the sinner cannot be His friend; and having within him the life that is not of God and interests that are diametrically opposed to His, he is not just one to whom God is a matter of indifference and who might, humanly speaking, be a matter of indifference to Almighty God, but is rather the enemy of God and one who looks on God as his enemy too.

Man was at war with God since the fall of our first parents. Our Lord came on earth to restore peace and friendship. To make man the friend of God and God the friend of man two things were necessary: man must be raised in some way to share in the life of God, and God and man must be once more united in the bond of mutual love. Jesus on the Cross is our peace, for in Him we have the life of God and in Him we love and are loved by the Father. In Him we have the life of God, since by His death He became the source of life to all that believe in Him: He was lifted up from the earth that He might draw all things to Himself and through Himself into the current of life that springs from the bosom of the ever Blessed Trinity. In Him we love the Father; for He is our Head, and that act of love whereby He accepted death that the world might know that He loved the Father, is ours too if we be united to Him. In Him are we loved by the Father, for He died for and in the name of every man who ever lived, and the love with which the Father gazed on the dying face of His well-beloved Son is meant to embrace every soul that mounts the hill of Calvary with his Saviour and bears Him company even to the shame of the Cross. He is our peace for He hath made both one—He hath made God and man one on the wood of the Cross, destroying the enmity that reigned up to that moment, in His own flesh, torn and bruised for us.

Christ is our Peace with the Father. But He is nothing the less our peace with our fellow man. Man may be, and has been, a wolf in his attitude to man. And what else was to be expected where man saw in his fellow a mere rival, one who symbolized just one more difficulty in the way of attaining even a minimum of pleasure, one whose gain was necessarily another's loss? Since Our Saviour died—and died for all men—our neighbour is flesh of our flesh and bone of our bone, being as he is co-member with us of the one mystical body. He is the booty of the King and Victor—the spoils carried off by Him in His triumph over sin and Satan. He is something that belongs to our Friend: "And you are Christ's" (1 Cor. iii. 23). He is not a rival, but a co-operator; working in organic union with us for the perfection of the body of which we are both members. His interests are ours. They can never clash. My growth in holiness is a gain to my neighbour, just as his growth is a gain to me, for whether it be he or I that grow, it is the life of Christ in us that develops, flowing from the head to the members and from member to member. And as the hand gains if the eye become more perfect, since the perfection of the eye will serve to guide the hand, so also one member of Christ Crucified gains if the other gain, for life can flow from member to member, always under the direction of Him Who is the Head. Christ is then the Peace of man with man. It is in Him that man finds his ultimate value, a value to be respected by every living creature; it is in Him that conflicting claims are merged into unity—into the unity of living members growing up into the perfection of a body whose blood flows from the wood of the Cross.

Besides the war of man with man there is waged on this earth a war no less terrible even if less visible: the war of fear with fear, passion with passion, flesh with spirit, that never ceases within the confines of the little world that is the individual. St Paul knew of this conflict. The law of his members fought against the law of his mind. He wished to do good, and found not how to do it. And this conflict of mind with flesh is not the only one that troubles the soul. There is the conflict of passion with passion. Our desires drag us at one moment in one direction, at another in a totally different one. Even at the same moment there may be in us a war of desires: while we follow one we are torn by the yearning to follow another. Our desires give us no peace, no rest. We have no rest from fear either. There is fear of failure if we hesitate and fear of failure if we are too impetuous. There is fear of failure if others interfere with us and fear of failure if we are left to our own resources. To all these warring hopes and fears and desires, to the war of flesh and spirit, Our Saviour has brought peace. Has not St Paul in the very passage where he bewails his sorry plight indicated whence he awaits deliverance? "Unhappy man that I am, who shall deliver me from the body of this death? The grace of God by Jesus Christ our Lord" (Rom. vii. 24–25).

It is Christ the Lord Who by His Victory over the flesh earned for us the grace to triumph in our turn in the struggle between flesh and spirit. It is He Who gives direction to our desires, Who gives them a goal. There can be no conflict of desires in him who adheres to his Saviour for all his desires are now centred on God; every fibre of his being feels the self-same urge, to draw near to the Father to Whom we have approach in His Son, Christ Jesus. There are no longer haunting fears; for the Cross is a sign in which one cannot fail to conquer.

Jesus was then the great Peacemaker. And were we but to consider for a moment the time-proved definition of peace, "the tranquillity of order", we could not fail to see that He must of necessity have been so. The reason is clear: He came on earth to restore the order, the harmony, that had been shattered by sin. God made the world and had seen that it was good. He had made Adam and had made him a balanced masterpiece of nature and grace. Sin entered in to shatter the harmony that was in the world and in man; and the loss of harmony meant the loss of grace. To restore harmony was to restore peace. It was to establish a new order of things in which the warring elements in man and outside of man would find possibility of conspiring to a common end. Sin had made man the enemy of God, and man could not find in creation a docile tool to serve his rebellion against the Creator. Man having rebelled against God found to his regret and shame that the instruments he sought to use to perpetuate his rebellion were themselves in revolt against him who had first set them the example of a refusal to obey. Nature—whether outside of or inside man—would never be at rest under man's dominion, unless he were to use it to return to and serve his God. Since man rebelled, it is a fact that even when restored to the divine friendship he has no longer the same full control over the material world that was his before the fall. But he can still have peace, on condition that it be the peace of conquest; the peace of the warrior ever on his guard, knowing that his trust in the strength of his arm and the loyalty of his allies is not unfounded.

God, in giving to man His Son, gave to him peace. The Crucified Saviour was the plan thought out by the Divine Wisdom for the peace of the world. Jesus was the incarnation of the divine plan of peace; He was the realization of what the Divine Wisdom had thought out. Jesus is then our wisdom. Our learning is the folly of the Cross. When St Paul spoke as he did of Our Saviour as "the wisdom of God" (Cor. i. 24), or when he says: "For although I be rude in speech, yet not in knowledge" (2 Cor. xi. 6) since he knows Christ and Him crucified, he indulges in no mere metaphor. Christ is the Incarnate Wisdom. He is the expression in human form of what God sees to be necessary for man. He is Divine Wisdom concretized in a human nature. Christ is our wisdom —He is all we know and all we need to know, and knowing Him we are truly wise.

Understanding in this way that Christ is the wisdom of God, we grasp the peculiarly profound sense of spiritual reality which prompted St Thomas to say that the gift which corresponded to the seventh beatitude was the gift of Wisdom. "Blessed are the peacemakers; for they shall be called the children of God." To be a peacemaker is to be like Him Who is our peace. To be like Him is to be a child of God; for the Father said of Him: "This is my beloved Son". But He is peacemaker precisely because He is Eternal Wisdom incarnate. We become peacemakers and sons if we, too, are full of the wisdom of God, of the Wisdom that is a gift of the Holy Ghost.

Our Lord was peacemaker because He, being the Eternal Wisdom, was Himself full of the peace of God. The gift of Wisdom makes us peacemakers, for it makes us to be full of peace and makes our peace radiate upon the whole earth. To be truly wise is to be at peace, for to be wise is to hold the key that unlocks all the problems of life. There is strife where there is opposition. But the man who is wise sees that all things have their harmony in God. He is at peace, for there is in him order, the cause of peace. He has understood that unless everything that is in him and everything that he touches be directed to God, he will live in the midst of chaos. For only God can reconcile all things; God alone is a goal to which all that is can be directed successfully. To direct life to a goal that is not God is to find that there are in life elements that do not fit, elements that are mutually destructive. To direct it to God is to catch up all that is in life into one vast and mighty stream whose powerful sweep and urge can bear along with it the motley flotsam and jetsam of human experience and human surroundings. And in that stream, and in its ceaseless flow, is peace; for its strength is disciplined and its mouth is the sea of Eternity.

He who is at peace in his own soul has the power of radiating peace. He has undone life's tangle for himself and knowing the secret can render a like service to others. Peace is in God and in His Christ. The peace-maker leads men to God through Christ. Elsewhere there is no peace. God alone, and His Anointed, know how to restore the harmony of the world. And the peacemaker will be called the child of God, for being a second Christ, his life is devoted to bringing his fellows to Him Who is their elder Brother. And he will be blessed, for he possesses the secret of God's Wisdom. He knows the truth, and the truth has brought him peace and joy.

It is but fitting that we should bring these few words on the gifts of the Holy Ghost to their conclusion by a reference to Him Who is the Way, the Truth, and the Life, Who is Our Model and in Whom is all perfection. Holiness is conformity with Our Lord. It is, what is still more, union with Him in the unity of one Mystical Body. We are holy when He lives in us, when He Who is holiness becomes the principle of our life and being. If the gifts of the Holy Ghost have a special significance for the spiritual life that can only be because in a special way they make us Christlike. That this is true of the gift of Wisdom has just been explained. It will be useful to indicate briefly that this holds also for the other gifts.

There is a striking passage in which the prophet Isaias speaks of the gifts: "And the Spirit of the Lord shall rest upon him: the spirit of wisdom, and of understanding, the spirit of counsel, and of fortitude, the spirit of knowledge and of godliness. And he shall be filled with the spirit of the fear of the Lord" (Isa. xi. 2–3). This is the only place in Holy Scripture in which reference is made to the gifts taken all together (the Vulgate version of the Bible is the only one which we are considering at the moment). Is it not significant that in this context the gifts are spoken of as virtues of the Messiah, and not directly as virtues of His followers? The gifts are in some way the peculiarity of the Messiah; it is they in their plentitude that give a truly distinctive character to what is human in Him. The gifts in us fill a similar role. They perfect our resemblance to Christ. The gifts are the gifts of the adopted child of God, given him that he may grow up into the likeness of Him Who is Son by nature.

To show in detail how the gifts were present in Our Lord would be matter for an entire work. Besides we have indicated from time to time when treating of the different gifts individually how examples of their working in Our Saviour may be found in the Gospels. Thus, we spoke of His Passion as an example of the action of the gift of Counsel. It is almost superfluous to add that the Passion is an example of the working of each and every gift. Wisdom is shown in the grasp of God's attitude to all that happened on the hill of Calvary; Understanding in the penetration of the inner sense of those texts of Holy Writ that needed as yet their fulfilment; Fortitude in bearing death; Knowledge in the grasp of the marvellous fabric of grace that was to be raised upon the wood of the Cross; piety in zeal for the interests of the Eternal Father; Fear of the Lord in that attitude of profound reverence that was Christ's when by His death He brought to its term the emptying of Himself begun at the hour of His birth in human weakness. And so it was through the whole life of our Saviour. All His actions were due to the impulse of the Spirit Who descended upon Him at His baptism and Who abode with Him at all times. The Holy Ghost is the Spirit of Jesus. When the Holy Ghost comes into our hearts it is as the Spirit of Jesus that He comes there. "God hath sent the *Spirit of His Son* into your hearts" (Gal. iv. 6). The Spirit is the Finger of the creative hand of the Father. If that Finger touch our souls it will be to outline in them the features of God's Son.

"Come Holy Ghost, that I may live, now not I, but Christ in me."

NOTE

In our treatment of the gifts of the Holy Ghost we have made explicit reference to our divinization by grace and the theological virtues, and to the need for something further—guidance by the Holy Ghost through His gifts—to enable the soul to live with a certain ease and assurance on the divine level. As it is but reasonable to enquire how the infused moral virtues divinize us and how their action is supplemented by that of the gifts, we shall touch very briefly on those points in the present note. Though the matter, in so far as it affects the gifts, has been treated adequately already in the body of the book, technical terms were avoided as leading to confusion. This present note is destined for those only who are interested in technicalities.

The theological virtues give us the power of exercising our activity on God as object. The infused moral virtues give us the power of acting supernaturally on objects other than God. But Faith and Hope need to be perfected in their mode of operation by the gifts of Understanding, Knowledge, Wisdom, and Fear, and this perfecting is the work of the Holy Ghost Who inhabits our souls by Charity and uses Charity and the gifts to perfect Faith and Hope. In just the same way the infused moral virtues, Prudence, Justice, Fortitude and Temperance, need to be perfected by Charity and the gifts.

Prudence gives us the power of determining a course of action in a supernatural way. The gift of Counsel enables us to do so with ease, assurance, and that apparently rash disregard of mechanical method which characterizes love's instinctive unerringness.

Justice gives us the power of paying what is due in the supernatural order. Piety perfects our justice by making every debt to be in our eyes a debt to a loved Father in Heaven.

Fortitude gives us the power of facing danger supernaturally. That Fortitude which is a gift adds on to the mere power a certain ease and unshakeable firmness born of love of God from Whom the danger attempts to separate us.

Temperance gives us supernatural restraint in our desire for gratification. Fear of the Lord (in addition to perfecting Hope) gives us a holy dread of any bond that would hinder our flight to God, and gives thus to our temperance that note of sensitive restraint characteristic of one who loves with generosity and has no room in his heart for any love but one only.

There is then a perfect parallelism between the action of the gifts on the theological virtues of Faith and Hope and their action upon the infused moral virtues. In each case the virtue—whether theological or moral—gives the power of acting: the appropriate gift gives ease and instinctive sureness. But it is, if we may so speak, nothing more than an accident that the name Fortitude should be common to both a gift and an infused virtue. The name is common, but the functions are distinct. Besides, something very analogous holds true for the other three infused virtues: for Counsel is the Prudence of him who gets and follows advice; Piety is Justice to a Father; Knowledge of one's weakness (Fear of the Lord) is the root of spiritual Temperance. The wonder then is not that one gift and one virtue should have the same name, but that the names of all four gifts should not have their counterparts among the virtues.